Praise for *Norwich*

"Crouse has written a powerfully inspiring and thought-provoking book filled with wisdom and counterintuitive insights. I couldn't put it down. *Norwich* is a refreshing and much-needed intervention that puts joy at the center of the parenting conversation."

—Amy Chua, bestselling author of
Battle Hymn of the Tiger Mother and *The Triple Package*

"A small gem of a book—a quiet Jeremiad about what's gone wrong in this country with the way we raise athletes into adulthood and a meditation on how we might begin to repair that broken process."

—Julie Checkoway, bestselling author of
The Three-Year Swim Club

"Both a brilliant book and a needed blueprint. Sports parents and aspiring young athletes can now, through this charming and revelatory story, follow the best and healthiest example. Crouse has performed the neat feat of providing both a terrific piece of reportage, and a public service."

—Sally Jenkins, bestselling author of
The Real All Americans

"Brimming with community-building ideas that transcend sports, this book challenges the current overextended, high-pressure world of youth athletics and provides the tools to help foster a positive, hometown-based alternative. Highly recommended."

—*Library Journal* (starred review)

"By the time readers finish Crouse's account, they may shift from wondering how Norwich does it to asking why everybody doesn't do it this way."

—*BookPage*

"Crouse's common-sense findings . . . are refreshing. Her book is a reminder that in an age that stresses winning at all costs, the true champions of the Olympic world are those who transition into lives as happy and productive adults. An inspiring story of a unique town."

—*Kirkus Reviews*

"The tremendous focus and sacrifice it takes to become an Olympian often leads to imbalance in life. The village of Norwich has shown that a strong community can foster love of sport and competitive success without sacrificing balance."

—Michael Phelps, 28-time Olympic medalist

"Crouse proves that there really is a town in which all the kids are above average—in this case, in a range of Olympic winter sports. Be careful Norwich. After reading this, the rest of the country will be headed your way!"

—Beth Kobliner, bestselling author of
Make Your Kid a Money Genius (Even If You're Not)

"Learning the backstory of each athlete is fascinating, as is Crouse's depiction of how the Olympics have changed dramatically over the course of her career. The book concludes with thoughts on creating Norwich's culture around the globe, making it a valuable read for parents, coaches, and teachers everywhere."

—*Booklist*

1984 Olympian Jeff Hastings, whose fourth place finish in the large hill was the best ever performance by an American-born ski jumper, now emcees Olympic send-offs for younger Norwichians.

Mike Holland, a two-time Olympic ski jumper who set a world ski flying record in 1985.

Three-time Olympian Hannah Kearney at a homecoming parade in Norwich after she won the gold medal in moguls in 2010.

SKI A

NORWIC

1 Mile from

1500 FT. RO

30 ACRES OPE

NIGHT S

Under Flood Light

Open Afternoons

Saturdays and

WARMIN

For Inform

all 653-M   White

Two-time Olympic runner (2008 and 2012) Andrew Wheating races through several inches of snow.

The first Norwich home-grown Olympian, Betsy Snite, a silver medalist in the slalom in 1960.

Brett Heyl, who competed in the men's kayak slalom singles in Athens in 2004.

Snowboarder Kevin Pearce was expected to contend for a gold medal in 2010 before he sustained a career-ending brain injury during a practice crash.

NORWICH

ONE TINY VERMONT TOWN'S

SECRET TO HAPPINESS

AND EXCELLENCE

KAREN CROUSE

Simon & Schuster Paperbacks

New York   London   Toronto   Sydney   New Delhi

Simon & Schuster Paperbacks
An Imprint of Simon & Schuster, Inc.
1230 Avenue of the Americas
New York, NY 10020

First Simon & Schuster trade paperback edition January 2019

SIMON & SCHUSTER PAPERBACKS and colophon are registered trademarks
of Simon & Schuster, Inc.

For information about special discounts for bulk purchases, please
contact Simon & Schuster Special Sales at 1-866-506-1949 or business@
simonandschuster.com.

The Simon & Schuster Speakers Bureau can bring authors to your live event.
For more information or to book an event, contact the Simon & Schuster
Speakers Bureau at 1-866-248-3049 or visit our website at
www.simonspeakers.com.

Interior design by Carly Loman

Endpaper credits: (Hastings) Jennifer Hauck/*Valley News*; (Holland) Nancie
Battaglia; (Kearney) Nicole Bengiveno/*New York Times*/Redux; (Wheating)
Courtesy of Betsy Wheating; (Snite) Associated Press; (Heyl) *The Charlotte
Observer* © 2008 McClatchy; (Pearce) Stan Evans Photography

Manufactured in the United States of America

1 3 5 7 9 10 8 6 4 2

Library of Congress Cataloging-in-Publication Data

Names: Crouse, Karen. Title: Norwich : one tiny Vermont town's secret to
happiness and excellence / Karen Crouse.
Description: New York : Simon & Schuster, 2018. |
Includes bibliographical references and index. Identifiers: LCCN 2017012269
(print) | LCCN 2017036896 (ebook) | ISBN 9781501119910 |
ISBN 9781501119897 (hardback) Subjects: LCSH: Sports—Vermont—Norwich.
| Sports—Social aspects—Vermont—Norwich. | Olympic athletes—Vermont—
Norwich. | Athletes—Vermont—Norwich. | Norwich (Vt.) —Social life and
customs. | BISAC: SOCIAL SCIENCE / Children's Studies. | SOCIAL SCIENCE
/ Sociology / Rural. | SPORTS & RECREATION / Olympics. Classification:
LCC GV584.V45 (ebook) | LCC GV584.V45 C76 2018 (print) | DDC
796.09743/65—dc23
LC record available at https://lccn.loc.gov/2017012269

ISBN 978-1-5011-1989-7
ISBN 978-1-5011-1990-3 (pbk)
ISBN 978-1-5011-1991-0 (ebook)

To Roderic, whom I nearly killed on a ski slope,
but who married me anyway,
and my father, James Crouse,
who is gone but never far from my thoughts.

CONTENTS

PROLOGUE

The road to the 2018 Winter Olympics in Pyeongchang, South Korea, runs through a pocket square of a town tucked between two interstates in the northeastern United States. Near the 89 and 91 interchange lies the town of Norwich, a hilly and wooded family-oriented farming community in rural Vermont. With a main street lined with white clapboard colonial buildings and a landmark steepled church, Norwich could be a set designer's rendition of a small New England village. It is a cartographer's challenge, barely registering on the map with its roughly 1,440 single-family households, including mobile homes, and a musty gymnasium contained within a brick meetinghouse. What it has in abundance is room to roam; Norwich is about a four-hour drive from New York City and two hours from Boston, but it's not all that popular as a second-home destination—the people who live there *really* live there.

Yet despite its apparent ordinariness, Norwich is home to a probabilities puzzle for the statistics students at Dartmouth College, less than two miles away as the hermit thrush flies.

This town of roughly three thousand residents has accounted for three Olympic medals, and, since 1984, has put an athlete on every US Winter Olympics team except one. Like a groundhog poking its head out of its burrow each February, every four years the Norwich athletes leave the cozy, caring cocoon of their small town for the glare of the world's grandest sporting stage.

The town doesn't lie fallow once the snow has melted; it has also sent two athletes to the Summer Olympics. In all, Norwich has produced eleven Olympians—an even dozen if you count the snowboarder Kevin Pearce, and the townspeople would never dream of overlooking Pearce, who sustained a career-ending head injury a little more than a month before the 2010 Winter Olympics, where he was expected to contend for a gold medal. To put Norwich's bountiful harvest in perspective, consider that Spain, with its population of 46 million, has won two Olympic medals in winter sports since 1936. New Zealand, home to 4.7 million people, majestic mountains that served as a backdrop for the Lord of the Rings film trilogy, and a wide range of adventure sports, has earned one Winter Olympics medal. In 2010, the freestyle skier Hannah Kearney became the first Norwich athlete to strike Olympic gold when she won the women's moguls in Vancouver. With her milestone achievement, she supplanted Bob Keeshan, the actor who played Captain Kangaroo on the eponymous children's television show, as the town's most celebrated resident. "Supposedly, one out of every 322 residents is an Olympian," Hannah said during those Winter Games. She added, "I don't know if it's the well water or what."

The well water in Norwich is perfectly delicious, but the town's outsize success in Olympic sports has more to do with the way it collectively rears its children, helping them succeed without causing burnout or compromising their future happiness. It's how harried parents across America would like to bring up their children if not for the tiger moms and eagle dads in their midst. The town has much to teach us about ensuring that our children grow up to live meaningful lives in both victory and defeat.

But before exploring the phenomenon of Norwich, let me make one thing clear: The town is not representative of the country as a whole. It is overwhelmingly white and mostly middle class, with a median household income of eighty-nine thousand dollars, well above the national average of fifty-six thousand.

With its population of professors and doctors, Norwich has the demographic—the wealth and the driven personalities—to be at the vanguard of the helicopter-parenting movement. And yet the town has largely opted out of the athletic and academic arms races being waged elsewhere.

Situated across the Connecticut River from Dartmouth College, Norwich used to be dismissed as a cow town by the people in Hanover, New Hampshire, where the university is located. The father of Norwich's first summer Olympian, kayaker Brett Heyl, who also grew up in the town, recalled many of his classmates, the children of farmers, showing up at school with manure on the soles of their shoes from mucking horse stalls. Such a scenario is unlikely now, but despite its growing affluence, Norwich has retained its bedrock agrarian values and rustic charm.

The children of Norwich still have the physical space and parental distance to explore, and discover, their place in the world. Its adults, generally speaking, have traded the acquisitive treadmill for daily nature walks and other grounding experiences. The residents look out for one another, and their connectivity provides a social safety net that no amount of money can buy. Numerous studies have shown that wealth and isolation are two sides of the same gold coin; the more money people have, the more cut off they feel from the friendships and support that can help them navigate difficult times. Niobe Way, a professor of applied psychology at New York University, told me that the social tapestry of Norwich represents a triumph of nurture over the natural order of the modern world, which has given us a wealth-and-acquisition model that favors autonomy over relationships and independence over community.

Norwich succeeds as a guide for overwhelmed parents—no matter where they put down their roots—on how to rear kids to be happy champions, resilient competitors, and contented, productive adults. Of course, not everybody conforms to the Norwich model; the town has its share of hovering parents. But almost by accident, the town has created a culture that seems to serve as the perfect incubator for developing the ideal Olympic athlete.

Its residents seem to have absorbed a saying passed down through the generations by farmers in the area: "Never going to make biscuits out of them kittens." The parents of Norwich are not inclined to try to mold their offspring into something they are not. They're taking their cues from their children, rather than conducting and scheduling their children's lives. As a result, the town has succeeded in preparing its athletes not just for professional achievement but for fulfillment in their post-sports lives. The Norwich athletes that I came to know seemed to have sidestepped the substance use, anxiety, and depression that often plague Olympians in retirement. Dr. Steven Ungerleider, a sports psychologist who has served in several capacities with the United States Olympic Committee, conducted a study, published in 1997, in which he interviewed fifty-seven retired United States Olympians in twelve sports. Forty percent of the group reported having serious post-Olympics problems. "Many reported that this was the only life they knew and it was inconceivable to do anything else," Ungerleider wrote. With one notable exception, the Norwich Olympians have managed this difficult transition better than most.

Jim Kenyon, a columnist for the local *Valley News,* described Norwich to me as "Disney World with maple trees." He would know. He brought up his family in town, and though he is no longer bound to the place by his children, now grown, Kenyon continues to live in Norwich, where his neighbors run the spectrum from mansion owners to yurt dwellers. That he pokes fun at the place but is in no hurry to leave is telling, as is the fact that the town's unofficial den mother is neither a coach nor one of its celebrated athletes. Her name is Beth Reynolds, the children's librarian at Norwich Public Library who tailors reading recommendations to each youngster's personality and whims. Even more than the athletes who compete all over the globe, it is Reynolds who opens new worlds to the children of Norwich.

Yet as extraordinary as the town seems, the seeds for its success can be planted and cultivated anywhere.

Norwich started producing Olympians at the advent of the television age. A young woman named Betsy Snite won a silver medal for America, and Norwich, at the 1960 Olympics in Squaw Valley, California, the first Games to be televised live in the United States. CBS aired thirty-one hours of coverage over the eleven days of competition. In 2014, when the most recent Norwich Olympian, Hannah Kearney, competed in her third and final Games, in the Black Sea resort of Sochi, Russia, NBC showed fifteen hundred hours over eighteen days. The town has had a front-porch seat to the rise of the commercialization and professionalization in the Olympic movement. Betsy retired from skiing shortly after the 1960 Olympics, and only then was she able to endorse and promote skiwear without fear of losing her amateur status. By the time Hannah arrived on the scene some forty years later, the model had changed. She was paid as a product endorser for clothing and ski equipment while she competed, but most of her sponsorships dried up after she retired.

Television turned out to be the Games changer. The exposure from global broadcasting partners attracted transnational corporate sponsors, which turned competitors into commodities and muddled the original message of the Olympics as a worldwide celebration of sport. I was reminded of how much the Norwich model matters when I returned home from covering the 2016 Summer Games in Rio de Janeiro. Several of my friends told me they hadn't bothered watching the competition.

They were over the Olympics as must-see TV and were talking about the event as if it were a reality show they had once enjoyed immensely but now found fraudulent. So many unsympathetic characters! So many farcical story lines! How could they root for athletes with cartoonish muscles who were likely to win medals only to later fail tests for performance-enhancing drugs? They expressed a nostalgic longing for the star swimmers and runners of their youth, who seemed more accessible and personable and less greedy and entitled. The consensus was that the Olympic movement was buckling under the weight of its excesses.

Norwich is why all is not lost. How can you not root for the ski jumper Mike Holland, who progressed from "a flying sack of potatoes"—a label slapped on him when he was an ungainly young jumper—to a two-time Olympian? Or Andrew Wheating, who found his way to the track as a high school senior and less than three years later ran in the Summer Games in Beijing? And what about Hannah, who overcame her aversion to backflips to become a trailblazing moguls skier? Mike, Andrew, Hannah, and the other Norwich Olympians went for broke in their sports but didn't get rich—and they didn't much care. The sports enriched their lives, and that was what drove them.

Norwich probably will not like that it has been made the subject of a book. This is a town with such an aversion to publicity that it tried to ground Mary Poppins. The Disney character may be perfect in every way, but several Norwich residents did not take to double-sided commercial banners for a 2015 holiday production of the musical with a spoonful of sugar. The signs appeared like a row of floating dominoes that stretched from the Ledyard Bridge one mile outside Norwich to the library in the town center. On an Internet community board, posts decried the banners as visual litter threatening the town's natural beauty, and a few people said they would boycott the production in protest. I talked to parents in Norwich who have banished televisions from their homes because they don't want their children to be exposed to commercials.

Norwich is a place with deep agrarian roots, and that still shows. The town was founded in 1761 as a farming community. While farmers were eventually replaced by doctors, academicians, and white-collar workers employed by Dartmouth and its hospital, Norwich remains true to the tenets set forth by the original homesteaders—hardworking people who did not manipulate their crops to make them turn out a certain way or try to accelerate the growth of their animals by injecting them with chemicals. Instead, Norwich's residents have simply made judicious use of the resources on offer.

In the nineteenth century, fortune hunters flooded the area as part of the Bridgewater gold rush, only to discover that the land did not lend itself to quick riches. Those who stayed found a way to make the flinty terrain bear fruit.

Over the past half century, the same has held true in the quarrying of Olympians. For the most part, the Olympians of Norwich did not sacrifice their childhoods by specializing in one pursuit to hasten their progress. They grew up changing activities with the seasons. The sports that offer the greatest exposure in America, and therefore the greatest potential for fame and fortune, are not the sports that typically capture the imaginations of Vermonters, who are known for their fiercely independent, contrarian personalities. The chain of Olympians includes no figure skaters, perhaps the most glamorous of the winter athletes. Instead, Norwich is brimming with ski jumpers and freestyle skiers throwing caution to the wind and pushing the boundaries of risk and reward. In their pursuit of excellence, the Olympians of Norwich collectively have overcome a broken back, numerous concussions, and scores of broken bones. Kevin Pearce sustained a brain injury forty-four days before the start of the Vancouver Olympics in a training accident that ended his competitive career. But it did not really slow him down. The subject of the 2013 documentary *The Crash Reel*, Pearce now fills his days with motivational speaking and working with his nonprofit organization, Love Your Brain, to improve the quality of life for those affected by head trauma.

The Norwich athletes know the risks involved in their extreme sports but are undeterred. Nearly three years after her Olympic gold-medal performance, Hannah sustained a bruised liver, two broken ribs, and a punctured lung in a training accident. She returned to competition three months after the October 2012 accident and finished the 2013 season by winning one of her six overall World Cup moguls titles. Like Vermonters who make the best of their unforgiving winter climate, the Norwich athletes accept that growth begins where one's comfort zone ends. Their fuel is renewable, and their drive was summed up by Hannah when she said, "A lot of satisfaction in life is cultivated by working towards a goal because you feel organically motivated and truly happy about your choices." Sage words, because in the end, few Olympians are able to cash in on their medals in what has become an oversaturated market. In 1960, when Betsy Snite became Norwich's first homegrown Olympic medalist, the Winter Games program included twenty-seven events. In 2014, when Hannah became the most recent, the program had grown to ninety-eight.

During my first visit to Norwich, I attended a reading by Deirdre Heekin, a local restaurateur, farmer, and author, at the town's two-story clapboard bookstore. There to promote *An Unlikely Vineyard*, Heekin read from a chapter that focused on the five factors she identified as key to farming success: geography, variety, climate, culture, and the individual. Heekin explained how the remaining farmers in the area produce remarkably successful yields through their canny use of the climate and location and their commitment to planting a rich variety of crops. They are considered a bit eccentric by the fresh arrivals from suburbia who can't understand the farmers' penchant for spreading their animals' manure in open fields near their property to fertilize the grasses or sleeping with a baby lamb born in the chill of winter to a mother who died or rejected it. And yet the farmers and the newer arrivals can both agree on the communitarian values that shape the town's athletes.

Heekin's descriptions carried me home to Santa Clara, California, in the early 1970s, where the air was fragrant with apricot blossoms from the orchards when we moved to the area when I was eight, my salesman father hoping to escape the work-first, family-second culture in Harrisburg, Pennsylvania's capital. Our arrival coincided with the beginning of the technology boom, which would fundamentally change the area through its nurturing of a culture that is all about new ideas and quick turnarounds and an achievement-based, money-oriented approach that ushered in an era of material acquisition. The city attracted newcomers intent on disrupting the status quo—to remake it, not perpetuate it. Today Santa Clara is the epicenter of the job-centered lifestyle. And while the families have shrunk (from 3.18 people per household in 1970 to 2.68 in 2010), the wood-and-stucco residences that cocoon them have become supersized. Where Craftsman houses once left dainty footprints on large lots, McMansions now sit shoulder to shoulder. The fruit orchards are long gone, and so is all the affordable housing that helped cultivate an expansive middle class. When I talked to people who lived in Norwich forty years ago, they bemoaned the disappearance of farmland, the appalling rise in house square footage, and the newly paved roads or streets renamed because, as one old-timer said with a sniff, "The original names sounded too country." But unlike with residents of Santa Clara, the changes they speak of remain essentially cosmetic. In Norwich, while people move in and out and existing homes get makeovers, the character of the place persists.

Norwich has its own police, fire, and water departments. Its downtown is anchored by a historic thirty-nine-room inn; a general store; and a post office, and includes a bookstore; a couple of fine restaurants; offices for architects, lawyers, accountants, and psychotherapists; boutiques; a hair salon; and Tracy Hall, the center of the town's operations. The surrounding terrain is hilly, and many of the locals like to turn their sloping backyards into bunny hills or beginner ski jumps. The closest major airport is a ninety-minute drive, and in the winter moose crossings and icy roads can make the journey feel like a settlers' crossing. The town is remote enough that it remains hidden except to those who are looking for it. I talked to townspeople who bought their homes sight unseen, so eager were they to put down roots in Norwich.

Dartmouth's relationship with the surrounding community is a model of how a well-endowed educational system can give back. Athletes and staff members volunteer their time to work with the youth in the area at a ski school that was started in the late 1930s by a Dartmouth graduate to introduce local children to the sport. The college-owned Skiway, which opened in 1957 and has more than a hundred acres of skiable terrain, was the childhood playground of all the Norwich Olympians but Snite. The university's forty-five-meter jump where Jeff Hastings and Mike Holland honed their skills as teenagers has been dismantled, but young skiers can still take flight at Hanover's Oak Hill, where Hastings and Holland continue to volunteer their time as instructors.

The Olympic athletes from the town don't seem in any hurry to leave. With few exceptions, when their competitive careers are over they unpack their bags and stay put, because they want their offspring to enjoy the same experiences they had. They join family businesses or hang their own shingles and serve as instructors on the side. By staying they become living monuments for the younger generations, who grow so accustomed to seeing Olympians in their midst that they consider the Olympics almost a rite of passage, right there with going to college.

The athletes of Norwich live side by side with ex-jocks, like the father I met during a recreational league soccer game who worked in New York's Financial District and in San Francisco before giving up his high-powered job to become a teacher. Clayton Simmers starred in lacrosse at his high school in Potomac, Maryland, and competed with distinction at Yale before earning his MBA at Dartmouth's Tuck School of Business. After college, he embarked on a business career with Merrill Lynch in Manhattan and worked for a start-up in San Francisco before moving with his wife, Susan, a fellow Tuck School graduate, to Norwich to bring up their two sons. He cheerfully allowed that he was underemployed, having decided the trade-off—less money but more time with his family—was worth it. His work as a third-grade teacher leaves him with time to coach lacrosse through the Norwich Recreation Council.

Simmers played multiple sports growing up, and he and his wife are in agreement that a well-balanced childhood is beneficial to their kids' overall development. They blend in seamlessly with the now-grown children of Norwich who left to attend college and start their careers, only to find their way home after they became parents. They accept the town's high taxes as the cost of having quality public schools and town services. Many work as telecommuters, setting up mobile offices in their cars in the library's parking lot to take advantage of a strong cellular signal and the library's Internet hot spot. Norwich is not a place that is tightly tethered to technology. Cellular and Internet connectivity remain spotty, which helps explain why many of the townspeople I talked to carried flip phones in their purses or pockets. Why buy a smartphone when its bells and whistles are effectively silenced by hills and forests? The townspeople have their favorite chat rooms and social platforms, but these are physical spaces—in the aisles of the general store, at the gym or downstairs meeting room in Tracy Hall, in the shops along Main Street.

Norwich does have a time-warp feel to it that extends beyond its potholed information superhighway. The town is listed on the National Register of Historic Places. And even in the coldest part of winter it is a warm place, with people inclined to treat strangers kindly. When a "Welcome to Norwich" sign was erected to greet travelers arriving from Interstate 91, Dartmouth, or the Appalachian Trail, it prompted grousing among a few old-timers who were of a mind that hospitality should be extended rather than advertised. The town's de facto chamber of commerce is the family-owned general store, Dan & Whit's, whose slogan could double as the town motto: "If We Don't Have It, You Don't Need It." The gathering spot has served as the site of at least three weddings, with Dan Fraser, who runs the store, officiating at a makeshift altar between the narrow aisles of flannel shirts and work pants. Teenagers in town looking for a part-time job know to reach out to Fraser, who will hire them to stock the shelves or work the cash registers. The store's currency is trust, with groceries added to a running tab that is paid off at the end of the month. For the town's poorest residents, the 6 percent who live below the poverty line, their debt, more often than not, is quietly forgiven.

Even though Norwich is relatively affluent, its model has always been one of equity. Nearly two decades before Dartmouth would welcome the first women into the freshman class, Betsy Snite, the town's first homegrown Olympian, grew up skiing alongside the college boys. The Ford Sayre program, where all the Norwich Olympians got their starts, was one of the first children's ski programs in the country, offering instruction to girls in an era when beauty still trumped brawn, as borne out by sports events that included pageants as part of the competition.

Norwich is also generous in helping neighbors who are less well off. It is the kind of place where a man dies and leaves his estate to the town with the condition that his money be used to ensure that no child endures a winter without a new pair of mittens. People contribute money for scholarships for drawing, painting, photography, and writing classes. Or they volunteer to flood the town green during the winter so that elementary school children can skate before and after school.

A local artist, Paul Sample, allowed part of his property to be used as a ski jump regularly frequented by Jeff Hastings, Mike Holland, and their brothers. The jump is overgrown now, but if you look hard you can make out the Bob Hope nose of a ramp. A ski run cut through the property where Betsy Snite grew up. The towline that carried the children to the top of the hill was powered by a Ford truck engine. Many a day of skiing ended with cups of hot chocolate and parents and children gathered around a bonfire toasting marshmallows. Goodrich Hill, Sadler's Hill, Lyle Field, and Booth Field were all places whose owners allowed the local children to traipse up and down their private property. Those ski playgrounds may be gone, but other traditions remain very much alive. Every Wednesday during the winter, the elementary school in Norwich still lets out early to facilitate family skiing. Children can ski alongside their parents or receive free instruction from Olympians. A mother of three told me that it is hard to steer her children away from the ski slopes when they have the opportunity to learn from the best.

Hump days were also the next best thing to snow days for Hannah Kearney, who chose her outfit for school with special care on Wednesdays. "I always wore something that I could change out of quickly," she said, the better to wring the most daylight out of her afternoon on the mountain. While her sport is increasingly populated by burnt-out gymnasts and divers who trade one obsession for another, Hannah embodied Norwich's adherence to nature's rhythms. She changed sports with the seasons. So did Tim Tetreault, a three-time Olympian in Nordic combined whose decision not to attend high school at a specialized sports academy paved the way for his world record feat as a senior at Hanover High in 1988. Tetreault teamed with a dozen of his classmates to break the Guinness world record for marathon leapfrogging, logging 888 miles over eight days of continual jumping in alternating shifts. Years later, when Tetreault included the feat in his résumé, he said prospective employers were more inquisitive about his role in the leapfrogging world record than his three Olympics.

As a town, Norwich bucks the trend toward single-sport specialization, the privatization of youth leagues, and the

Darwinian view of youth sports that normalizes cutting all but the most skilled players. Even now in Norwich, recreational teams don't have cuts, affording every youngster the chance to participate in any sport. Having spent my journalism career observing the antics of win-at-all-costs coaches while wedged in the bleachers alongside parents micromanaging their children's play, I was not prepared for my first recreational-league soccer game on the town's fields at Huntley Meadow. On the crisp autumn Saturday morning that I spoke to Simmers and his wife, their son scored two goals in quick succession. After his second score, the coach motioned the boy over to the sideline and told him it was time to take a breather. He substituted another player for the boy, and neither parent challenged the decision. They just continued talking to me as if their son getting pulled from a game after scoring two goals was perfectly normal. I witnessed zero parents yelling at the coaches or the referees, but kayaker Brett Heyl discovered a much more intense environment when he volunteered to officiate youth soccer games while living in the Washington, D.C., area. He absorbed so much verbal abuse from parents on the sidelines that he eventually quit.

Norwich has a deep aversion to pushing its children too hard too soon. The public high school limits the number of

Advanced Placement courses. And during one of my visits, the local paper, the *Valley News*, ran a front-page story in which teachers called for further reducing their high school students' stress, in part through independent study and special projects. The town's climate, both the literal seasons and its collective values, fosters an unhurried approach to life. The speed limit on the main road through town is 25 miles per hour, and a furor erupted on the community Internet message board when speed bumps were installed on one road near the hiking trails to foster the safe coexistence of cars, joggers, dog walkers, and bicycle riders. Underlying the argument against the speed bumps was the belief that any commuter who found the posted speed limit too restrictive is perhaps better off living somewhere faster paced. Norwich's steadfast encouragement, and the support offered without judgment, provides the perfect platform for the kind of risk taking that launches innovators like Kevin Pearce and Hannah into the great unknown.

Now is a good time to revisit Norwich's well-balanced athletes. The billions of dollars spent to broadcast events like the Olympics has turned sports into big business. The rise of all-sports TV networks has created mass exposure where there once was little for events like the Little League World Series or high school football, causing the pro model to trickle down to youth sports. The stars of championships who used to draw scant public attention become overnight sensations, little pros in training. While researching this book, I heard about third graders from a state bordering Vermont who are required to sign contracts stating they would choose soccer over any conflicting activities on game days. I read about teenage pitchers who are blowing out their elbows because they are throwing too much, too hard, too soon. In their efforts to help their children earn an athletic scholarship, make a US Olympic team, or turn pro, scores of parents now treat sports like law or medicine—as another prestigious profession to be pursued with a singular focus. Parents and coaches should strive to develop the next Jim Holland, younger brother of Mike and a two-time Olympic ski jumper who took the skills he honed in his sport—discipline, determination, perseverance, and goal setting—and applied them to starting a successful business. In 1996, he cofounded backcountry.com, a Utah-based online retailer that specializes in outdoor clothing and equipment. The president of the San Francisco–based strategic equity investor that bought the company in 2015 lauded its "strong brand heritage and authenticity." In other words, the company was a reflection of Jim, who was, in turn, a reflection of the town that shaped him.

Norwich restored my flagging faith in Olympic sports.

By 2014, as I muddled through the mess that was the Sochi Olympics, with its displaced citizenry, disappearing dogs, dilapidated accommodations, and distressing price tag, my emotional tether to the competition was fraying. It was my ninth trip to the Olympics—tenth if you count the 1984 Summer Games in Los Angeles, where I volunteered as a hostess—and it was hard not to feel as if I was witnessing a grande dame's last, gasping breaths. The Sochi Olympics rolled up a record tab of $51 billion and required a large army of police to secure. Russia gave the world an Olympics characterized by human-rights violations and a systemic doping program by the host country. The Games were also marred by a handful of serious injuries to participants who were encouraged to take on ever-higher degrees of risk for the entertainment of the viewers.

Where were the Olympians who were in it for the joy? Hannah Kearney's remark about the well water wasn't so far off. Norwich does have an old-fashioned tonic to cure what ails contemporary sports. Like their farmer forebears with their crops, the parents of Norwich learned through trial and error the best methods of nourishing happy athletes; by valuing participation and sportsmanship, and stressing fun, community, and self-improvement. This is the story of how they did it.

1

SKI PATROL

Lesson: *Teach Your Parents Well*

Norwich's Olympic tree took root with the Snite sisters in the 1950s. Betsy and younger sister, Sunny, were the Lillian and Dorothy Gish of Alpine skiing: performers without voices. The early specialization, parent-driven medal-or-bust model that has become a pesticide in the soil of contemporary sports—it was all there on the backyard hill of the two family properties on Hopson Road, where Albert O. Snite groomed his daughters to be champion skiers.

Their unhappy legacy would shape how at least one Norwich parent nurtured his child. The extent of the sisters' heartache was unknown to me when I set out on Sunny's trail. My letter of introduction came back unopened with "Refused" and "Return to Sender" scrawled across the front of the envelope in spidery handwriting. No one who had grown up with Sunny was surprised. They had not heard from Sunny in decades. They talked about her as if she were a hothouse flower long dead.

For several weeks, Sunny clouded my thoughts. She had once been the subject of magazine articles. How and why had she become a recluse? Her former classmates, now in their seventies, described her as a ghost, but how many apparitions have a landline? Whenever I called the number I had dug up for Sunny, I got a recording of a girlish voice expressing bemusement that she had been found. The voicemails I left went unanswered. While pondering my next move, I received a call from an unfamiliar number in Texas. The woman on the other end of the line introduced herself as Maria Lyle, the second of Sunny's two children. She had been enlisted by her mother to interview me before Sunny would agree to entertain my questions. Our conversation was my first inkling of the extent to which a grown-up Sunny had gone to avoid her past. With Maria's help, I made contact with Sunny, and a meeting was arranged at a spot near Sunny's home, many states removed from Vermont. On the appointed afternoon, the woman who greeted me in the parking lot of the rural Italian restaurant several miles outside Missoula, Montana, had the stooped carriage of someone weighed down by her life's choices. Her face was tanned and weathered, and her wispy white hair was gathered in the back with two combs. Happiness may have eluded her, but the decades hadn't extinguished the mischief in her eyes.

She hadn't been back to Norwich in more than thirty years, not since a short, disheartening trip to see her father some time before his death in 1982. She assumed she wouldn't be received well, but my conversations with people who had known her convinced me otherwise. Over soup and pasta, the seed for Sunny's return to Norwich was sown. It took several months to schedule a date of travel, and even after the details had been worked out, she was hard to pin down. Less than a week before her scheduled departure, I received a text from Sunny's daughter, who would be traveling with her, warning me that I shouldn't be surprised if Sunny backed out. She could not shake her reservations about what kind of reception awaited her in Norwich. After failing to leave her mark on the sport that dominated her childhood, Sunny presumed that the townspeople shared her father's profound disappointment in her.

Until 2010, Betsy was the only Norwich resident to grace an Olympic medals podium. But to the community the sisters left behind, Betsy's silver medal in Alpine skiing came at too great a cost. Like the alcohol on Betsy's breath in her later years, her unhappiness as an adult could be masked but never really covered up. And Sunny ended up poorer for trying to ski her way into her father's heart. "He was the epitome of the parent who was pushing his kids," said Brett Heyl's father, Mike, whom Sunny babysat when he was a child. A man who dated Sunny in high school told me that Al didn't know how to relate to his daughters except as female versions of himself. "Al would have been better off having sons," the ex-boyfriend said ruefully. Had it been up to Sunny, she would have spent her childhood on a saddle, not skis. "I wanted the horses more than the skiing," she said. They had an artist neighbor, a man named Paul Sample, who kept horses on his property, and Sunny watched the animals with a deep yearning. She felt as tethered and bridled as they were. She repeatedly asked her father if she could have a horse; a relative in Illinois even offered to send a thoroughbred to Vermont for her as a gift. Sunny told her father she would be willing to give up ski racing to care for it, but her father would not hear of it. You are going to ski, he told her, "come hell or high water." A disconsolate Sunny would regularly climb a maple tree on the family's property, and from her perch she would gaze at Sample's animals. She may have thought she was hiding, but one day Sample rode by on horseback, stopped at the tree, and squinted up at the spot where Sunny had wedged herself. She thought he was going to scold her for being a busybody. Instead, he told her that he was going away for six months and was looking for someone to care for his horses. Would she be interested? Sunny could hardly contain her excitement. Her father told her she could care for the horses, but only if she was diligent about her skiing. It was a hard bargain for Sunny, but worth it. Those months around the horses formed her happiest childhood memories.

It would be difficult to grow up in Norwich when the Snites did—or even now—and not give skiing a try. Geography exerts a pull nearly as great as gravity. If the sisters had been reared in Santa Clara, California, a decade later, swimming probably would have been their sport. If they had been raised in Southern California after that, tennis likely would have been their game. But they were from Norwich, situated across the Connecticut River from Dartmouth College, which in 1928 hosted the first slalom race in the United States. It didn't matter how rich or poor you were; skiing was accessible to all children in the area through an innovative program called the Ford Sayre Memorial Ski School.

Ford Sayre, a Dartmouth graduate who was running a lodge with his wife, Peggy, started a junior ski school to stimulate business in the slow winter months. On becoming the manager of the Hanover Inn, next to the Dartmouth campus, he expanded his ski school in the late 1930s to include children of the guests and also local youngsters from farm families, who might not otherwise be exposed to skiing because of its expense. He encouraged participation by girls, whom he noticed were often assigned domestic chores that kept them indoors during the long winters. He was adamant that the female descendants of strong women like Ann Story, the widow with five children whose work for the colonists earned her the moniker "The Mother of the Green Mountain Boys," should not be ignored. (I would learn about Story while reading a chapter of a biography on her to a class of Marion Cross third graders at lunchtime, an activity that adults in Norwich are encouraged to do.) The Memorial Ski Council was created with community donations after Ford, an Army Air Corps captain, died in 1944 in an airplane crash during a war bond drive. His widow carried on his mission of making ski opportunities available to every child, not just the advanced racers or natural athletes. The children were encouraged to view success through the prism of progress; to improve was to win. That it became a laboratory for Olympians like Betsy and others was entirely incidental. In an environment that stressed the social aspects of skiing, the Snite sisters, with their world-class competitive ambition, were outliers.

In truth, the outlier was their father, Al. He was one of the founders of the Ski Council and served on the board in its early years, when his daughters were part of the program, but rejected the program's low-key approach. He had grandiose goals for Betsy and Sunny. "He wanted them to become the next Andrea Mead Lawrence," said Mike Heyl, referring to the Vermont native and three-time Olympian who in 1952 became the first US Alpine skier to win two gold medals in a single Winter Games. Al's concerted focus on his daughters becoming champions did produce success, but it was fleeting. Cars were a hobby of his, and with his daughters it was as if he took Ford Sayre's gender equity and souped it up like one of his classic automobiles. While Sunny and Betsy appeared outwardly robust, they sputtered and stalled as a result of his tinkering.

In addition to Betsy and Sunny, Al had another daughter, Elizabeth, from his first marriage. She lived in Los Angeles and was a few months younger than Betsy, whom Al adopted when she was a toddler after he wed her mother. Elizabeth would spend her summers in Norwich with Al, who would accompany her to the tennis courts and critique her game as she played. She was an adult before she recognized her good fortune in not being another vehicle for Al's reconditioned ambitions.

The realization allowed Elizabeth to make peace with his cameo role as her father. "I was a little blessed that I could look at it from the outside in," she said. Why was Al so invested in his children's athletic activities? Elizabeth believed it was inextricably tied to his childhood diagnosis of diabetes. Considered at the time a potential death sentence, the disease severely restricted the activities in which he was able to take part. Elizabeth said her father's involvement in Betsy's and Sunny's sporting lives grew out of his forced inactivity. He projected his competitiveness onto them, with mixed results. Betsy shared her father's fierce desire to win, while Sunny was more of a free spirit who enjoyed the serenity of the outdoors. In 1956, a seventeen-year-old Betsy was the youngest member of the US team for the Winter Games in Cortina, Italy. She raced in the giant slalom but did not finish. Four years later, Sunny had an outside chance of competing in her first Winter Games at the same age. Because Betsy had reached the world's stage as a teenager, Sunny was expected to do the same.

The pressure Sunny felt was stifling, but she grew adept at presenting a cheerful front. She was all smiles in a photo essay that appeared in the January 1960 issue of *Seventeen,* the monthly magazine aimed at teenage girls. The piece identified her as a "17-year-old member of the United States Olympic women's ski squad," her manifest destiny committed to the page. In fact, by the time the magazine hit the newsstands, she had been dropped from the list of Olympic hopefuls. The description of Sunny as an Olympian was not accurate, but then, neither was the scene of her seated around a table with a group of classmates enjoying a fondue dinner. Sunny's father discouraged her from having friends over to their house and frowned on her socializing with her classmates. One of her friends from the photo, Elise Braestrup Wellington, sat next to Sunny at a different table decades later, during Sunny's New England home-coming, and said the magazine photo had been staged. She couldn't recall Sunny participating in any school clubs or social outings because she was preoccupied with ski-related activities, including a daily run that took her past Elise's house. The description of Sunny as "a full-time seven days a week skier" was the single truth in the photo essay. The Snite sisters were admired by the boys and girls with whom they grew up, but none envied their lives. They didn't understand what Betsy and Sunny gained from their myopic focus on skiing. From the outside, the competitions in faraway locales might have radiated glamour, but it was the era of the amateur athlete. The Olympics were several years away from creating overnight stars and instant millionaires. Skiing in Norwich, then as now, was regarded as an activity meant to offer a lifetime of pleasure, not a lost childhood.

Betsy was skiing between bamboo poles when she was a small child, while Sunny was on skis before her third birthday. Her first time, Sunny snowplowed straight down the hill with her poles tucked behind her as she gathered speed, oblivious to everybody's panicked shouts to turn. She was headed straight for a barbed-wire fence until a Dartmouth student—one of the hill's regulars—skied over and scooped her up.

In the 1950s, skiing was sweeping the nation. The invention in 1934 of the rope tow and of the chairlift two years later helped the sport take off in remote American mining villages like Aspen, Colorado, and pristine mountain terrain like Sun Valley, Idaho, which soon became the first winter destination resort built in the United States. Both inventions made skiing less laborious, conserving the time and energy required to climb the side of a mountain before enjoying the exhilarating payoff of the descent.

Skiing was no longer the province of the wealthy few with the financial means to travel to the top resorts in Europe, and its growth attracted many of the best teachers from the continent. They came to the United States to spread their knowledge and passion in places like Dartmouth, where the shorthand for their instruction became a running joke: "Bend zee knees, two dollars, please." The 1940s and 1950s produced the first generation of US winter athletes, led by Andrea Mead Lawrence and Gretchen Fraser on the women's side and Billy Kidd on the men's, capable of competing against the best skiers from Europe.

Because Norwich and Hanover were not close to any

resorts, the children of the area were introduced to skiing in its purest, most stripped-down form, away from the glitz and glamour of the winter havens. By the time they were in elementary school, the Snite sisters were familiar figures at the neighborhood skiing spot. Known as Altow, or Cemetery Hill because of the gravesites, including that of Ford Sayre, that freckled the face of the hill, the slope featured a three-hundred-foot drop and a rope tow on Elm Street powered by a noisy Ford V-8 engine. The local children would return empty soda bottles at Merrill's General Store, the precursor to Dan & Whit's, and use the deposit money for the all-day skiing fee of fifty cents, which went toward paying for the gas used to run the rope-tow engine. Because of its affordability and accessibility, the hill was popular with everyone from pint-sized beginners to the Dartmouth College men's ski team. The coach in that era was Walter Prager, a Swiss Alpine skier who became Hanover's Father Winter. His tenure at Dartmouth lasted from 1936 to 1957, and in that span he put more than a dozen athletes on US Olympic teams. He designed and built Dartmouth Skiway, which would become the second home of every Norwich Olympian. Prager's success provided the blueprint for Al, who watched over the slope like a snowy owl.

Al and his second wife, Elizabeth, known as Betty, both taught skiing at Ford Sayre, with Betty working mostly with the smaller children. Betty was a statuesque beauty who, like Al, was always impeccably groomed. She busied herself with her household and deferred to her husband when it came to her daughters' activities and discipline. Al had ample time on his hands. Unlike the other fathers in town, he did not toil in the fields or commute to a nine-to-five job in the shiny Cadillac that completed his dapper image. Al and Betty radiated wealth. A woman who grew up in Norwich with Betsy and Sunny said the Snites were regarded as "the rich people in town." But then, it was an era, she said, where maintaining appearances was a full-time job. On Dartmouth alumni forms, he listed his occupation as the vice president of the Chicago-based Imperial Credit Company, which Sunny described as the family business. Al lacked neither the funds nor the free time to indulge his passion for his daughters' skiing. He yanked Betsy and Sunny out of school, sometimes for months at a time, so they could train in Colorado and travel throughout the United States and, later, Europe, chasing good snow and better competition. In his enthusiasm, Al seemed snow-blind to the fact that his daughters desired a more normal adolescence. They were allowed some of Norwich's typical childhood pleasures. In the summer, they played tennis and swam with the neighborhood kids—but only after their training was done. Sunny said they tried field hockey at Hanover High, but none of her classmates remembered them playing any other sport. They distinctly remembered that after the fall, the Snite sisters would disappear for months, as if abducted by winter. Al supplemented his daughters' skiing workouts with three-, five-, or seven-mile pre-breakfast runs through town, which they grudgingly completed while wearing weight bags, sewn by their mother, around their ankles.

Sunny had her favorite shortcuts but worried that a neighbor would catch her trimming miles off her route and tattle on her to Al. Not that anyone did. The other parents noted how Al pushed Sunny and Betsy and advised their children to show compassion toward the sisters. A woman who grew up near the Snites recalled a rare visit to the Snites' home for a playdate with Sunny when the girls were in grade school. She became anxious when she saw padlocks on a few of the kitchen cupboards and the refrigerator. Why would anybody keep food under lock and key? When she returned home, she told her parents what she had seen. Her father counseled kindness. "He said there are probably some issues there and to just be a friend to Sunny," she said. The townspeople kept whatever reservations they had about Al's methods to themselves. How he chose to rear his children was none of their business, and besides, Al did not socialize with them. He preferred the Dartmouth social set.

Ahead of his time in recognizing the importance of upper-body strength in the girls' ski-racing success, Al enlisted a neighbor and former national champion gymnast at Dartmouth, Lauren Sadler, to oversee strength exercises and weight-training programs; his daughters dutifully, if not enthusiastically, attended the sessions. In the summer, Lauren set up mats and other apparatus on the Snites' front lawn, and Al invited other children to join the girls in their "play." The neighbor kids may have thought they were engaging in spontaneous fun, but they were bit players in Al's show, there to provide extra incentive and competition for his daughters. Every exercise had a purpose. Years later, Sunny would read aloud a quote from Betsy from a newspaper clipping that she pulled out of a thick file on the sisters at the Norwich Historical Society: "I was extremely tunneled into skiing and nothing else existed for me." That sounded about right, Sunny said.

After Betsy's death at forty-five, her husband was interviewed by the *Valley News*. He described Al as "quite a taskmaster" and said he once asked Betsy why she adhered to the rigorous training schedule. "Dad told me if I didn't continue to train, he'd take my skis away," she said. The more she accomplished, the more loved she felt by her father. If she didn't ski, who would she be?

To her father, Sunny was Betsy-in-waiting, a designation no kid sister would relish and one that a headstrong Sunny often tried to mule kick. Sunny told me that she wished her father had steered her and Betsy into a team sport—perhaps allowed them to play field hockey all four years of high school. She longed for the embrace of the Norwich community.

Because she followed her father's rules to the letter—at least within his sight—Betsy became his favorite. Sunny was more querulous. She described herself as the black sheep of the family, a description others who knew the sisters said was accurate. No matter how hard she tried, Sunny could never surpass Betsy, who skied as if she had burst through the screen of an instructional film. A grade-school classmate, Rusty Sachs, described Sunny as "a ballerina on skis" who floated through a slalom course. Betsy, he said, was more like a race car driver, using her quick reactions to attack the course, always on the edge of losing control.

At her second Olympic Games, in Squaw Valley in 1960, Betsy's aggressiveness was her undoing in the downhill. She was skiing well when she crashed after losing her edges near the finish on a stretch fittingly named "the airplane corner." In the slalom she won the silver, and she just missed the medals podium in the giant slalom with a fourth-place finish. Betsy's friend and rival, Penny Pitou, won two silvers in what Penny rued was "the last of the small Olympics." The athletes were not yet familiar faces, as was made comically clear to Betsy and Penny at a pre-Olympics cocktail party held to honor the US Alpine team. One guest approached the athletes and asked brightly, "Do any of you kids ski?" And yet the beginning of the results-oriented culture that would eventually turn Olympic athletes into volatile commodities was there in the newspaper dispatches about Betsy and Penny. Squaw Valley was the first Winter Olympics on US soil since 1932 in Lake Placid, New York, and it didn't matter that the United States had produced only two Olympic Alpine gold medalists to that point. At Squaw Valley, it was expected that America's exceptionalism would be reflected on the podium. After Pitou won her second silver, she returned to the Olympic Village with her head held high, only to be cornered by then Vice President Richard Nixon, who told her how sorry he was that she had lost. In the *Valley News*, a columnist writing under the name of Arthur Mountain wrote a piece implying that Betsy and Pitou had disappointed the country by failing to win gold. Several indignant readers wrote to say they were proud simply to see one of their own represent Norwich on the international stage. It was a view that Norwich residents would echo decades later about another Norwich skier, Hannah Kearney.

Betsy retired soon after the Squaw Valley Olympics in what felt like a reprieve. Her ambivalence toward skiing leaped off the page in a *Sports Illustrated* interview she gave in the lead-up to the 1960 Olympics. Betsy was portrayed as an attractive young woman who enjoyed being set loose in the Alps, where handsome male skiers from Austria appeared around every bend, and where her father, described in the story as "an ardent and often very vocal ski fan," was notably absent. She viewed practice as a chore. "When it's time to race, I'll be ready," she said in the article. "In the meantime, I'm going to have fun." The skiers who knew Betsy at that time described a hard-partying, pack-a-day smoker who liked to drink and preferred jitterbugging the night away to getting a good night's sleep to be fresh for training. Betsy enjoyed racing, but she wasn't fond of practicing. She could get away with not training because she was so skilled. Her slalom technique elicited comparisons to the men. All the time she spent skiing with—and learning from—the Dartmouth team members gave her a competitive advantage. "She was probably the best technical skier I've ever skied with," Penny said.

At Dartmouth, which had an all-male student body at the time, the skiers referred to Betsy affectionately as their mascot. The kid-sister kindness they showed her was apparently not the norm. More than a dozen years later, the actor Meryl Streep was one of sixty women invited to spend a term on the campus. In a 2000 interview, Streep, who arrived at Dartmouth in late 1970 from Vassar College, described an "us-and-them feel to campus" and said the male students "really didn't want us there."

The gender wars were only one of the conflicts in which Betsy found herself in the crosshairs. She came of age as the Cold War between the United States and the Soviet Union was heating up. After the Soviet Union joined the Olympic family in 1952, the sports pages became another kind of battleground in the global conflict between democratic capitalism and totalitarian communism, with the femininity of the American athletes held up as a triumph against the mannishness of their Eastern European counterparts. Betsy's natural beauty was remarked upon in most stories in which she was mentioned. She was always perfectly coiffed, and on the slopes she carved clean lines, but like a swan on a lake, there was a lot going on beneath the placid surface. Betsy's self-worth was wrapped up in her hourglass figure, which won her the male gaze, and her skiing results, which earned her the adoration of her father. The pressure to maintain her figure and her championship skiing form left Betsy anxious. Nicotine and alcohol took the edge off. Penny Pitou often roomed with Betsy on the road and grew accustomed to being awakened in the middle of the night by the smell of smoke from Betsy's cigarettes. Once, Penny said, Betsy took a few puffs from a starter's cigarette before launching herself out of the gate to race. Pia Riva McIsaac, an Italian ski racer, said she once asked Betsy if her smoking compromised her stamina. Betsy said she didn't know about that, but it definitely calmed her nerves.

Betsy's other race-day rituals included applying fresh

polish to her fingernails. She never missed a chance to emphasize her femininity, telling reporters that her favorite part of European competitions was the après-ski tea dances and that her goal was to get married, settle down, and have a family. She was selling her womanhood to the smitten; in February 1960 *Sports Illustrated* published a story on the US Olympic women's Alpine ski team. But only one of the squad members—Betsy—graced the cover. Years later, Sunny grew reflective as she studied the cover portrait of her sister. For so many years she had envied Betsy's natural beauty and her skiing results without stopping to consider the cost to her sister of upholding the image of the feminine athletic ideal. "She looks so sad," she said. "It kind of makes me wonder if she really had a choice to ski, either."

But at the time, Sunny found it difficult to summon any sympathy for Betsy. She often felt as if her first name was a cruel joke—because of Betsy's radiance, mostly, but also because Sunny had made her entrance into this world in November 1942 during a blizzard. She never felt as if she could match Betsy's brilliance on skis, her ease in social settings, or her bombshell figure. Joan Hannah, a two-time Olympian and a teammate of Betsy's on the 1960 US squad, said Al's preference for Betsy was so obvious that she naturally assumed Betsy was his flesh and blood and Sunny the adopted daughter rather than vice versa. "Betsy did everything her father wanted," Joan said. In pushing Betsy and Sunny to be *the* best rather than encouraging them simply to do their best, Al exacerbated their sibling rivalry by creating a zero-sum competition between his daughters. As the Betsy-in-waiting, Sunny thought any resentment was hers to shoulder alone. Then I showed her a newspaper clipping. Asked in the story if Sunny sought skiing advice, Betsy replied that she did so constantly. "She's a typical sister, if you know what I mean," Betsy said. Sunny read and reread the quotes. She giggled and clapped her hands in delight. "Perfect," she said. It hadn't dawned on Sunny until that moment that being the older sister with the tagalong sibling might have been its own trial. As an adult, Sunny's contact with Betsy was limited to occasional phone calls. She did not attend Betsy's wedding or her memorial. "I wasn't invited," she said. And so in search of some connection to the sister who had been unknowable to her, Sunny asked during her New England visit to be driven to Stowe, Vermont. Located roughly eighty miles from Norwich, Stowe is where Betsy spent the last twenty years of her life. Our first stop was supposed to be the

Vermont Ski and Snowboard Museum, housed in an 1818 building that once functioned as the town hall, but it was closed. We parked, and Sunny walked in and out of shops along Main Street. She asked every clerk or cashier, most of whom had not been alive when Betsy died, if they knew of Betsy. Sunny was looking for pieces to fill in the puzzle that was her sister, but nobody was able to help. She stopped by the chamber of commerce, where Betsy's name failed to elicit any recognition—this despite her inclusion in the Hall of Fame wing of the museum. Sunny had come to collect remembrances of her sister. She left with a pile of brochures on the town's attractions. We exited the town center and headed toward Mount Mansfield, stopping at the address where Betsy's sports shop had been located. A wine-and-cheese store stood in its place.

Sunny's desire to know more about her sister's life took her to another town, this one seventy miles from Norwich, where she had more success. In Laconia, New Hampshire, Sunny sat for lunch with Penny Pitou, whom she hadn't seen in more than fifty years. Penny had enjoyed the kind of sisterly relationship with Betsy that Sunny never did. After their skiing careers were over, Penny said she asked Betsy regularly about Sunny. Betsy's stock reply was that she didn't know where Sunny was or what she was doing. How could that be? "Sunny didn't just fall off the face of this earth," Penny would say to Betsy. "So where is she?" Betsy never seemed to care.

The lunch with Penny gave Sunny much to digest: How much of the sisters' disconnect was the inevitable result of their different personalities, and how much of it was created by their inorganic childhoods? Sunny was shy and less comfortable in social situations than her gregarious and glamorous sister. The girls' classmates would describe Betsy as sophisticated and very social. Their depiction years later of Betsy rang true to Sunny, who twice refused to join her sister on the racing circuit in Europe, despite her father's urging and financial support, because she didn't want to have to live up to Betsy's example on the slopes or at the mixers afterward. "There was too much pressure from guys to be Betsy's little sister, to behave like she did," Sunny said.

Betsy lived for her soirees in Europe. Training and racing overseas emancipated Betsy from her father, affording her a measure of independence she didn't have at home. Between her Olympic debut in 1956 and the next Winter Games in Squaw Valley, she steadily improved by training alongside Austrian men in the Alps.

She collected boyfriends and trophies like stamps and visas in her passport. She needed the boyfriends to get the trophies because they helped her improve her skiing skills. The Austrian men would take off from the top of the mountain, and Betsy would follow in hot pursuit. "You learn to ski fast," Betsy said, "or spend a lonesome winter." She chased after one Austrian in particular, Josl Rieder, six years older than Betsy and also an Olympian. He accompanied her to races in the United States, waxed her skis, and advised her on strategy, taking on many of the roles typically filled by her father. Betsy, who grew up Episcopalian, converted to Catholicism because of Josl. She hoped they would be married, but sobriety was the one conversion she could not make for love. Josl pleaded with her to stop drinking, and when she didn't, he said, it doomed the relationship. Her skiing compatriots doubted the union would have lasted regardless. They could not imagine the independent, high-spirited woman they knew finding contentment as an Austrian innkeeper's wife.

After the Squaw Valley Games, Betsy briefly returned to Norwich and spent the rest of the winter working with the young skiers at Ford Sayre, where an annual award would be established in her name after her death. And then she was gone. Except for trips to visit her father, she was rarely seen in Norwich after that. She had no childhood friendships to ground her. They had been sacrificed to skiing. "She was just floundering," Penny said. Betsy would struggle with alcohol addiction for the rest of her life. Penny recalled occasions when she could not understand her friend's slurred speech over the phone. When they got together, Betsy would insist that she was drinking honey tea, but Penny wasn't fooled. She knew the mug contained something stronger.

A month before the 1984 Winter Olympics, Betsy was among the honored invitees at a celebration in Woodstock, Vermont, for the fiftieth anniversary of the first rope tow in the United States. Five months later she died at the Medical Center Hospital of Vermont of lung cancer. She was forty-five. While living in Norwich, I came to know the town's unofficial historian, Bill Aldrich, who was born in 1937, one year before Betsy. As children they skied together, and in the fourth grade, Betsy became his first girlfriend. He took her to a dance at Tracy Hall, where she wore a tulip corsage made by his mother and sister. Bill said that it was common knowledge among those who grew up with her that Betsy had taken her own life because she didn't want to repeat her mother's drawn-out death. But the Vermont certificate of death indicates otherwise, stating her cause of death as a brain hemorrhage caused by a clot that traveled from her lung. Penny and her husband were on their way to the hospital to be at Betsy's side when she passed away.

One of Penny's everlasting regrets is that she never staged an intervention, but Betsy and Sunny's other sister, Elizabeth, doubts any such efforts would have made a difference. She recalled a conversation that she had with Betsy a few years before her death in which she spoke as if the best part of her life had ended when she retired from skiing. Imagine, Elizabeth said, feeling as if your life began to decline when you were twenty-one years old. Betsy was never able to change how she saw herself, how her father saw her. Her identity was as a performer, not a person. She was hired by Bogner to sell skintight skiing stretch pants and by DuPont, which employed her as a skiwear consultant. With Josl out of the picture, Betsy looked for love closer to home. In 1964, she was married in the Catholic church to Bill Riley, the head of the news bureau of Stowe's Mt. Mansfield Company, which operated the local ski resort.

Long before the Vermont Ski and Snowboard Museum moved to the town, Betsy served as a living, breathing, schussing monument to the small state's outsize success in Olympic sports. Her public persona as a champion skier required Betsy to maintain an effervescent countenance, but her friends sensed a deep reservoir of loneliness. Betsy skied recreationally. She took up golf, playing six times a week when the weather allowed, and whittled her handicap to single digits. In the 1970s, she opened the Betsy Snite Ski & Sport Shop, which she and her husband ran. She never had the children she had hoped would fulfill her, and her fractured relationship with Sunny precluded any bonding with her sister's children.

In April 2017, Betsy and eleven other athletes were inducted into the Vermont Sports Hall of Fame for their contributions in bringing exposure and recognition to the state. During the banquet, held in Burlington on a cold, rainy Saturday night, Marilyn Cochran Brown, an Alpine skier who competed in the 1972 Winter Olympics, was chosen to accept the award on Betsy's behalf. She began her speech by saying she wasn't sure why she was standing in for Betsy. "I didn't know her really well," Cochran Brown said, adding, "She was a very private woman."

Penny Pitou had encouraged the event organizers to contact Sunny about attending, and they did reach out to her. Sunny took a few days to consider the offer and warmed to the idea of sharing with a sold-out crowd some of the sentiments she wished she would have expressed to Betsy before she died. "I could finally give Betsy the tribute I couldn't while she was still alive," Sunny told me when we spoke by phone. Our connection was not great, but I could clearly make out the regret in her voice. "I always believed we would connect as sisters in our later years," she said. "Then it was too late."

Sunny was at home in Montana recovering from shoulder replacement surgery and a fire that reduced her home to ash when her sister was honored in Vermont. Circumstances had conspired against her, and not for the first time. In 1959, ahead of her senior year at Hanover High, she was named to the eleven-woman US national team from which the six-woman Olympic squad would be chosen. When I asked Sunny decades later if she had been a strong candidate for one of the last Olympic berths, she was circumspect. "That was the gossip" was all she would say. Al took Sunny out of school during the fall of her senior year—just as he had done with Betsy four years earlier—so she could focus her time and energies on skiing. There was no part of their lives that he did not oversee. He prepared his daughters' skis before races, sometimes staying up all night to apply the wax. He acted as their publicist, arranging for a photographer to take studio-quality posed shots of Betsy and Sunny for publication in the local paper. One ran in the *Valley News* two months before the Olympics, the sisters posed side by side on a winter-white incline. The photograph was staged, Sunny said. By the time it ran in late December, she would be out of the sport—for good.

In November 1959, shortly before her seventeenth birthday, Sunny was skiing with other national team members in Loveland, Colorado. The training sessions were informal; the official workouts didn't start until the beginning of December. Sunny remembered the weather being glorious. "Perfect snow, a perfect blue-sunshine day," she said. She took off after a member of the US men's team, hoping to catch up with him so they could ride up the chairlift together. There was a steep pitch toward the end of the run, and Sunny took a bump hard, slid off the course, and crashed into a tree. Her back was ablaze in the cold. She had sustained three microfractures in her lower spine, but they did not show up on the initial set of X-rays. The pain was intense, her agony made worse by the rumor, spread by Betsy, that she was not really injured but was merely seeking attention.

Sunny could have recovered and tried for the 1964 Olympics. Penny Pitou considered Sunny a genuine talent, well positioned to make the next US team. She still would have been young—only twenty-one. But when she stepped away from the competition, Sunny experienced a kind of catharsis. She took a job as a hostess for a ski magazine that entertained clients during the Squaw Valley Olympics. Sunny said she paid scant attention to the competition. To be out of the Olympic conversation, she said, "was a huge relief."

As a journalist, I've encountered athletes who've attributed reckless behavior to a deep-rooted sense of shame. Some experienced trauma as children. Others felt powerless to express their desire to quit their sports— or at least to take a break. I knew a swimmer who celebrated her mononucleosis diagnosis because she was finally able to rest on doctor's orders. Could it be that Sunny subconsciously sabotaged the skiing career that made her anxious and unhappy? When I posed the question to Sunny, she said she'd have to think about it. She never offered an answer. If it was deliverance from skiing that she desired, Sunny got it. After the accident, she vanished. Fifty-five years would pass before Penny saw Sunny again.

When Sunny finally returned to Norwich in 2015, she was amazed by the warm welcome she received from the townspeople she had known as a child. On her first night back, Sunny sat around a kitchen table with class-mates who traded stories about her between mouthfuls of lasagna—made from ingredients donated by George Fraser, the patriarch of Dan & Whit's and a school friend of hers. Sunny's childhood friends talked about her as the sweet-tempered tomboy with the wind-chime laugh. They recalled her gathered around the television in the family's guest house with other teenage girls during Elvis Presley's first appearance on *The Ed Sullivan Show* and pointing her finger in disgust at Presley's swiveling hips. They remembered ducking under their desks to-gether during the air-raid drills at the Norwich elemen-tary school. They recalled watching her ski on Cemetery Hill or run past their houses and feeling a visceral pride that she was going places, a belief corroborated by the newspaper stories they read about her skiing successes. "And then all of a sudden," one of her classmates said, "you disappeared."

Sunny's memories of her childhood were fuzzy, the result of decades of practiced forgetting. The one ves-tige of her adolescence that she carried into adulthood was the back injury that ended her skiing career at seventeen; it has disrupted her sleep since. As she listened to people paint a picture so different from how she saw herself through her father's disappointed eyes, Sunny realized Al had perhaps been a poor judge and jury. If she had been allowed to have a normal adolescence, would she have embarked on adulthood with a more confident self-identity? The table fell silent when Sunny said her primary aim in 1960 hadn't been to make the Olympic team. It had been to graduate from high school with her class. "And have memories," she said.

Sitting in the front seat of a rented sedan, Sunny struggled to find her bearings as she was driven through town. It was the first time she had laid eyes on Norwich since a brief stopover in the early 1980s. She took note of the homes that stood where farmland once stretched. But subtle differences also caught her eye. The stone walls in front of a few of the houses did not appear to have been formed from stones excavated while clearing the land and haphazardly thrown together in a pile. The walls she pointed out looked carefully arranged to exude informality—like someone who spends two hours primping to achieve a casual look.

The Snite sisters' skiing careers were built like the

walls that Sunny dismissed as artifice. To outsiders, their development may have looked natural. But anyone in Norwich who had grown up with the sisters could see Al's handiwork. Sunny's childhood friends described Al as stern, tough, rigid; a taskmaster. Sunny called him complicated.

During her return to Vermont, she spent an afternoon at Dartmouth's Rauner Special Collections Library poring over files of newspaper clippings, yearbook pages, and other papers. It was a scavenger hunt, with every piece of information Sunny found on Al a clue that brought her closer to understanding the man whom she still called Daddy. After her back injury, he sent her to live with friends in California to finish high school. The academic year had started later there, so she could more easily make up the months she'd missed. That was the story that Al told Sunny, anyway. The truth, which he kept from her and Betsy because he didn't want their skiing to suffer, was that their mother had been diagnosed with cancer.

In May 1960, Sunny received a phone call telling her to come home because her mother was dying. It was the first she knew her mother was sick. After her mother's death, Sunny was overcome by grief. She was mourning so much more than the loss of a parent: a potential Olympic berth felled by a tree, and no discernible social life beyond the pages of *Seventeen*. After her mother's memorial, Sunny laid to rest the daughter that her father had cultivated from Norwich's hilly contours. She escaped Vermont and enrolled at the University of Colorado. She dropped out before the end of her first year to embark on the first of three marriages.

She had two children before her twenty-first birthday. She said all three of her husbands were abusive. Her daughter, Maria, didn't know her father, Sunny's first husband, but said she witnessed the abuse meted out by the third. Each time a marriage ended, Sunny's father provided minimal financial support but never said the words she longed to hear: Come home. He died without having met any of her husbands or either of her children. She blamed herself for their estrangement. "I quit college, I didn't make good marriages, I wasn't doing the right things in my life," she said. Sunny rarely skied with her children, who didn't know until much later that she had once been an Olympic prospect.

Sunny's third husband introduced her to long-haul driving, and she joined him on the road. Her freight included cattle and swinging sides of beef in refrigerated trucks. She had two CB handles: Bamm-Bamm, after the superstrong son of Barney and Betty Rubble from *The Flintstones* animated television series; and Carry Nation, after the American woman at the fore of the temperance movement. After the marriage ended, she remained on the road. The long-haul trucking life accommodated her desire to leave the past behind and think no further into the future than the next stop. She applied the discipline and focus her father drilled into her during ski training to stay alert through long stretches of lonely road. For the first time in her life, Sunny felt like she could choose her own path.

After she left the road for good, she settled outside Missoula in a double-wide trailer on twenty-three acres of land, most of it in a floodplain. While she was with her daughter in Missoula in late 2016, the trailer burned to the ground in an electrical fire. Sunny spent several months living with Maria and her two grown granddaughters in their Missoula apartment. She yearned to return to a ramshackle RV she keeps on her property, where she has an abundance of open space and as many horses for neighbors as people. She is intent on keeping the outside community at an acre's length; three gates stand between the edge of her property and her front door. "The way I grew up," she said, "how can it be any different?"

To those who gathered to welcome her back to Norwich, Sunny was hardly recognizable. Their only frame of reference for her was as a world-class performer. Her body had gone soft, and in conversation she veered into one thought and then, without warning, weaved into another, as if to avoid a multisentence pileup. It was sometimes hard to follow her. Her classmates would later tell me they struggled to reconcile the lithe and self-confident athlete they remembered with the woman who seemed unsure of her next sentence. Priscilla Weldon, one of her childhood friends, told a story about a teenage Sunny who talked Priscilla's parents into allowing her to join Sunny at a horse-riding camp. Armed with brochures and self-confidence, she delivered a presentation that won them over. Sunny grew quiet as her former classmates described a girl she barely recognized. "I'm speechless," she said.

Twenty-four years would pass before Norwich produced its next Olympians, ski jumpers Jeff Hastings and Mike Holland—whose parents, while supportive, allowed their talents to develop organically. The Snite sisters produced wonderful ski results, but no one in town wanted to raise their children to be like them. Sunny babysat for Mike Heyl when he was young, and even as a small child he could sense her unhappiness. Mike remembered Al being overbearing with both of his daughters, especially rebellious Sunny, and vowed that when he became a parent he would never cross that sometimes blurry line between encouraging and pushing. Mike's only child, a son, Brett, grew up to become the first child of a parent reared in Norwich to compete in the Olympics, at the 2004 Summer Games in Athens.

Betsy's success established Norwich as a place with favorable conditions for raising a champion skier. Many towns, including some smaller than Norwich, have produced Olympians. One is Easton, New Hampshire, population roughly three hundred, the birthplace of the Alpine skier Bode Miller, a six-time Olympic medalist. But what makes Norwich special is the people's connection to nature and one another, which blazes the Olympians' paths to happy adulthoods. The Norwich culture, with its organic cultivation of the whole person, promotes success in sports and life because one is never sacrificed for the other.

If the Snite sisters' lives had been woven into the town's fabric, Norwich might have provided a cushion for them when they stumbled. As it was, none of the other Norwich Olympians knew anything about Betsy except that she was the first. After Betsy's husband died in 2010, a few boxes filled with the couple's personal belongings, including their wedding album, ended up at the Vermont Ski and Snowboard Museum in Stowe. The volunteer curator who took possession of the items was saddened to think that there were no other custodians of their memories.

Betsy's story certainly wasn't passed down as an aspirational tale. In 1971, in a personal letter to a friend, the widow of Ford Sayre bemoaned the results-oriented environment that was blooming elsewhere. She could not reconcile that model, with its fancy uniforms and year-round training and faraway competitions, with her late husband's simple goal of making skiing available to all children. His vision was never intended to identify the best athletes. The goal was to instill in children a love of skiing that they never outgrew.

Much has changed since Betsy's silver-medal performance at the 1960 Olympics. Al's approach has been copied everywhere, it seems, but in Norwich. The Snite sisters reminded me of others I've seen over the years whose careers appeared to be ultimately harmed by a par-

ent's too-tight embrace; athletes like the swimmer Dagny
Knutson, who grew up in Minot, North Dakota—as unlikely a place to cultivate an Olympic swimmer as Norwich
would seem for an 800-meter runner. Knutson's father, a
former college football player, orchestrated every aspect
of her training from grade school through high school. He
steered her into a dry-land weight program when she was
ten and worked overtime to pay for trips to Florida and
California so she could test herself against better competition. Dagny would later say of her swimming that
she grew up feeling like a passenger along for the ride. It
was only looking back that she realized she could have—
should have, really—been in the driver's seat, dictating
the route. As a teenager, she set an American record in
the 400-yard individual medley, which marked her as a
prime candidate for the 2012 Olympics. "By high school
I had stopped hanging out with a lot of my friends," she
said. But Knutson never made it to the 2012 Olympics.
She didn't even make it to the US trials. While the 2012
team was being finalized, Dagny was receiving treatment
for an eating disorder. "Sometimes when I look back at
myself in high school, and the years I had the most success, I don't want to say I was clinically depressed, but I
wasn't genuinely happy," she said.

Unlike Sunny, Dagny twice tried to make a comeback but couldn't separate the pressure of performing from the pleasure of competing. She retired again, deciding she preferred to pursue friendships instead of championships.

Starting at the Norwich reunion, Sunny also seemed intent on making up for lost opportunities to socialize. Toward the end of the evening, she reached out to her classmates from Norwich in a gesture that might have made all the difference in the world had she acted sixty years earlier. "I'm collecting hugs," she said.

2

NORWICH'S AIR FORCE

Lesson: *It's Not About the Survival of the Fittest;*
It's About the Survival of All of Us

On one of those biting, pewter-sky January days that makes a Vermonter fantasize about the beckoning alabaster white beaches of Florida, Mike Holland stood in the gymnasium at Marion Cross Elementary, his favorite room in the school as a fidgety child. He was wearing the uniform of Norwich: khaki pants, hiking shoes, and a sleeveless down vest over a long-sleeve flannel shirt. Mike still had a boyish glint in his eyes as he explained the art of ski jumping to a class of fifth graders. He told them about growing up around the corner from the school in a two-story clapboard colonial on Church

Street, and how he got started in the sport in the fourth grade. Mike, trim and fit in his fifties, is a retired Olympian with a full-time job in finance, but he still finds the time every year to visit Marion Cross and deliver a ski-jumping presentation that is more fun than recess.

The students spilled into the gym and found the floor divided into three stations. The first stop consisted of drills using props like agility ladders and balance boards. At the next stop, the exercises emphasized jumping from a standing start and off a wooden bleacher. Finally, there was the pièce de résistance, a jump simulator that Mike designed and built, making practical use of his degree in mechanical engineering from the University of Vermont. The contraption—a rectangular board on wheels atop rails on an incline—would not have looked out of place next to a bounce house and face-painting station at a kids' carnival. Mike's daughter Greta, a fifth grader, was in the morning's first class, and he called on her to demonstrate how the device worked. She possesses the fine technique that he didn't develop until he was much older, but ski jumping, an Olympic sport for women since 2014, isn't Greta's passion. After the briefest of dalliances with basketball, she locked on to Alpine skiing, and he was fine with that.

Greta scampered up to the top of the board, bent at the waist so that her back was straight enough to balance a small carton of chocolate milk without spilling, bent her knees, extended her arms behind her, palms up, and looked straight ahead like an old-fashioned swimmer on the starting block. She nodded to her father, who disengaged the lock. Greta rolled down the rails and then soared, ponytail flying, onto a pile of foam mats. She bounded off the pile and shuffled to the back of the line, watching and clapping as the other kids took turns launching themselves into the air, many of them tentatively, with their brows knitted in concentration. After landing on their stomachs on the mats, the students rolled over and giddily regained their footing. A few exhaled in relief. Every child got two jumps, and Mike's daughter snuck in a third before moving with her group to the next station.

The exercise gave the youngsters a sense of how it feels to take flight. Their questions gave Mike an inkling of what might be keeping them earthbound. One asked, "How do you land without breaking your legs?" Another wondered how long jumpers are in the air. Mike explained that the landing is the easiest part because it is not a straight vertical drop; the jumpers set their skis parallel to the angle of the slope and touch down, catlike, with one foot in front of the other and knees bent to absorb the shock. And the jump is over in a blur, easily less than ten seconds, though it can feel like an eternity. The kids exchanged awed looks. Class after class filed into the gymnasium, and Mike repeated his presentation with no loss of verve. One girl showed excellent technique on the jumping machine, sailing through the air like an arrow. She beamed when Mike praised her. He told me later that the girl had tried ski jumping but chose to concentrate on other sports. He shrugged. In keeping with the Norwich culture, the kids are mostly left to their own devices—just as Mike was.

At the beginning of each session, Mike showed a promotional video that included a grainy clip of his career highlight. The footage was from the World Championships in 1985 in Planica, in what was then Yugoslavia, where Mike soared the equivalent of more than two football fields. He flew 186 meters, or 610 feet. He was the first American to exceed six hundred feet, and also the first American jumper to set a world record. His record didn't last long. Matti Nykänen, the Michael Jordan of Finland, so cherished in his homeland that his likeness graced a postage stamp, surpassed Mike's mark twenty-seven minutes later. But Mike had made history, and nobody could take that away from him. Every time he watches his record jump when he is out spreading the gospel of ski jumping, the hairs on his neck stand at attention. When he talks to the youngsters about the sport, they want in. By lunchtime, he had received two dozen informal commitments from children whose hands shot up when he asked who would like to try his winter jumping program two nights a week under the lights at a hill near Dartmouth. But selling the kids on the sport is the easy part. The challenge is obtaining permission from parents who view ski jumping as a hospital visit waiting to happen. A teacher at the school told me about the year every child in her daughter's class expressed interest in joining the Ford Sayre program where Mike volunteers; only her daughter was able to secure a parent's written blessing.

Whenever Mike gives his presentations, he loses a half day of work but gains something more precious— the satisfaction of giving back as part of Norwich's decades-long daisy chain. His wife, Heidi, playfully chides him that in the winter he devotes more time to his volunteer ski instruction than he does his paying job. Mike pleads guilty. In January or February, it is not unusual to find him at Oak Hill in Hanover ahead of a youth practice conducting business with investors or developers on his mobile phone while he packs the snow with his feet. He can't help himself. This connection to the community—the giving and receiving of support—has sustained Mike since childhood. Norwich's geographic isolation fosters close-knit ties among the townspeople. The athletes are no different. It is not a coincidence that most of the Olympians of Norwich still live and/or work in town and will probably retire there; the daisy chain links are not easily pulled apart.

Felix McGrath, a 1988 Olympian in Alpine skiing, lives thirty-five hundred miles away but remains rooted to Norwich in spirit, extending the daisy chain across the Atlantic Ocean to Norway. McGrath, a Hanover High product who finished thirteenth in the giant slalom at the Calgary Games, has exported the Norwich way, applying the philosophies that shaped his childhood to his club coaching. Perhaps the best natural athlete of Norwich's Olympians, McGrath was a four-sport standout through high school, participating in soccer in the fall, skiing in the winter, tennis in the spring, and baseball in the summer. He advocates the same generalized approach to sports with his Norwegian skiers, encouraging them to avoid specialization until age sixteen. "Too many junior ski programs are too specific to their sport at a young age," Felix said, "which makes the sport too competitive at a young age, which in turn pushes out the multisport athlete." And that is a shame, he said, "because most child skiing stars at age twelve never make it to the top."

Felix, a five-time national champion, organizes his training groups by age, not ability, because that is the model he was exposed to growing up. Throw the most skilled children together, regardless of age, and you create a climate where only a few thrive, he said. And when kids are skiing with others their own age, they are more likely to form friendships. "You create the group environment, which is the key to having fun," said Felix, who worked as an instructor at Waterville Valley in New Hampshire and coached at the University of Vermont before moving to his wife's homeland in the early 2000s.

Mike became a ski jumper because a neighbor kid passed on his equipment and his enthusiasm. That boy—Mike's first model for the Norwich way—was Jeff Hastings, eighteen months older and already bitten by the jumping bug when he lugged a pair of heavy jumping skis over to the Hollands' house. Jeff, who had started jumping at eight, had outgrown the equipment. Sharing is a given in Norwich. So Jeff rang the doorbell, asked for

Mike, dropped the skis at his feet, and said they were for him. "You really need to try this sport," he said. Mike, who was ten years old and small for his age, looked at the bulky skis with skepticism. At the time, he preferred cross-country skiing. But he also admired Jeff and didn't want to disappoint him. "I really wanted to impress him and get his approval," Mike said. So he followed Jeff up the hill, to the Norwich property of the artist Paul Sample, who had groomed a twenty-meter jump on his land that he allowed kids to use in the winter. The boys stopped at the top of the incline, and Jeff helped Mike snap on the skis. "Okay," Jeff told him. "Now we're going to jump." Mike peered over the tips of his skis and gulped. He pictured himself tumbling down the hill, gathering speed like a human snowball. He stood there for several minutes, summoning his nerve. "When you're at the top of the hill, it just looks like a cliff," he explained to me. "You cannot see the landing until you're in the air." Finally, Mike pushed off. He wasn't in the air long, but he landed on his feet with his heart in his throat. "I was like, 'God that was scary,'" he said. His next thought was, "Let's do it again."

It was 1972, and ABC's weekly sports anthology program *Wide World of Sports* was using a spectacular ski-jumping crash as part of its introductory montage.

Vinko Bogataj was the Yugoslavian jumper tumbleweed-ing into America's living rooms every Saturday, and his agony-of-defeat crash became for many parents the first, and lasting, image of the sport. United States ski-jumping officials, mindful of how unnerving the wipeout was to watch, tried in vain to persuade the network to exclude the image from the opening. They argued that it was stunting the sport's growth. Mike's parents certainly had their reservations about ski jumping, especially his mother, Barbara, who was terrified of heights. But they didn't stand in his way. They averted their eyes and let their son pursue an activity that quickly became a pas-sion that he would pass on to his two younger brothers, Joe and Jim. It was something I often saw in Norwich—parents nurturing their children's enthusiasms no matter how culturally uncool, unfamiliar, or downright danger-ous. Jeff and Mike loved that Bogataj's wince-inducing crash was on a weekly loop for several years. They thought it gave the sport and those crazy enough to love it a cer-tain mystique. Decades before extreme sports came into vogue, ski jumpers were part of the first wave of adren-aline junkies. Mike would compete through concussive crashes that knocked him out and resulted in a dozen bro-ken bones, but he would also collect five national titles.

His early results wouldn't show it, but Mike was built for flight. He stopped growing at five foot ten inches and a feathery 152 pounds. But perhaps more important than his physiological edge was his parochial advantage: he was able to train every day alongside Jeff, two inches shorter and, in the early years, twice as successful. Everyone in the Dartmouth Skiway program benefited from being around Jeff. They saw how hard he worked and that his efforts were rewarded, which was highly motivating. Jeff and Mike were part of a culture that created self-driven kids who existed harmoniously with one another. That they became Olympians was fantastic but almost incidental to their self-discovery, independence, and relationship building. "It was really unique," said Jeff's younger brother Chris. "If you ever went off a ski jump, you were in the tribe."

The tribe helped its newer members overcome their fears. In the third grade, Tim Tetreault was petrified to launch himself off an eighteen-meter jump at Oak Hill, even though he would have been soaring only about five feet above the ground. He inspected the hill like an explorer who had stumbled on a new and vaguely threatening territory. Over and over he skied the landing hill to grow accustomed to the jumping gear and the contours of the terrain. The coaches did their part to help him over-come his fear. The jump was built into the side of the hill, and they'd devised an on-ramp at about the ten-meter mark so that Tim could start from there. But the last night of the jumping season arrived and he still had not been able to launch himself from the top. Determined to see Tim end the winter on a high note, one of the older athletes offered him a dollar bill if he jumped. The finan-cial incentive did the trick. Tim made the first exhilarat-ing jump and squeezed in a few more before the end of the night. "That thrill sustained my interest in ski jumping; it's what brought me back," said Tim, who would go on to jump from seventy-meter hills and grace three US Olym-pic teams in Nordic combined. Forty years later, he could remember as if it were yesterday the feeling of excitement and achievement upon making that first eighteen-meter jump. He said if it hadn't been for the encouragement from the coaches and other athletes that first winter, he might not have experienced any of the thrills or interna-tional travel that the sport made possible. The Norwich jumpers could serve as a model for social science research-ers, who have consistently found that positive relation-ships enhance not only performance but also physical and emotional well-being.

Early on, Mike could match Jeff's work ethic if not his results. His jumps lagged behind those of Jeff and his brothers, Brad and Chris. "They were especially good when they were young, and I was especially bad," Mike said. He would carpool to meets with the brothers in the Hastinges' wood-paneled station wagon, chauffeured to and fro by the brothers' father, Paul. On the return trip, he would be the only one without a trophy in his lap. He finished consistently last in the standings. Mike didn't appreciate it at the time, but he was building resilience. And back in Norwich, no one paid much attention to the results. The people in the town saw only that Mike clearly loved the feeling of being airborne. In those moments, it was as if an unseen force held him by the belt loop and whisked him into the cold, open air.

Jeff and Mike were both jumping for the pure joy of it. They certainly weren't motivated by money. Both had to work summer jobs to defray the expenses that piled up every winter as they traveled the world for competitions. Their intrinsic drive produced external success that snowballed, resulting in a decade-plus chain of US champions. Jeff and Mike inspired three of their brothers, Joe and Jim Holland and Chris Hastings, to compete, and they all became Olympians. Just as Jeff had ignited and fueled Mike's interest, Mike was there to be his siblings' guide. "We always had the focus of let's together do everything we can and share everything we learn to try to be better," he said. Not all of their training took place on skis. In the summers, the boys would jump off the roofs of their houses and leap over bars and boxes that they set up in their backyards. It may have looked as if they were misbehaving, but this unstructured play strengthened their leg muscles. They turned everything into a good-natured competition—even timing their drives from Norwich to Lake Placid, where they practiced at the jumping facilities, to see who could complete the trip in the shortest time. Jim Holland set the one-way record for the 136-mile commute, which typically takes three hours, in two hours, seven minutes, and fifty seconds. Long before they became national champion jumpers, they were familiar to the police patrolling the route.

In 1980, eight years after taking up the sport, Mike tried to jump his way to Lake Placid. It was the first Winter Olympics on American soil since the 1960 Squaw Valley Games, where the participants had included Norwich's first homegrown Olympian, Betsy Snite. At the US selection meet, Mike finished back in the pack, while Jeff missed a berth by two spots. Jeff did make it to those Lake Placid Games as a forejumper, enlisted to set the tracks for the participants ahead of the competition. At this stage, Mike was still making more of an impression with his ungainly form than his results. In the air, one ski strayed to the side, and he appeared to be dog-paddling with his hands. His awkward style earned him the nickname "The Flying Sack of Potatoes." "I can distinctly remember the coaches laughing at me as I jumped," Mike recalled.

After 1980, Mike and Jeff pushed each other to become the best jumpers in the United States. They corrected flaws in each other's techniques and were each other's biggest cheerleader, driven to get better together instead of vying for domination. Because of their Norwich upbringing, they recognized the value of relationships and did not regard them lightly or toss them aside in the pursuit of success. They thought everybody was like that until they showed up at training camps featuring athletes from all over the country and realized that the Norwich way was not the universal model (years later, the snowboarder Kevin Pearce would have the same experience, prompting him to cultivate his own merry band of travelers composed of friends who were also snowboarders).

At home, Jeff and Mike trained with the Dartmouth

jumpers, from whom they learned much. The college athletes changed the trajectory of Mike's career by introducing him to mental imagery. They encouraged him to visualize a jump in vivid detail over and over so that by the time he executed the jump in real life it felt as if he had already done it. Mike devoured books on the power of the mind, written by specialists in the emerging field of sports psychology. Some of his competitors made fun of him, but Mike didn't care. He realized that mental imagery was an unproven science. But it made sense to him. A person could achieve anything that the mind could perceive. It was like ski jumping itself—a leap of faith. Slowly but surely, through his work on the mountain and in his mind, Mike transformed himself from a flying sack of potatoes into vichyssoise. "Mike was a lot of raw talent who became an elegant ski jumper," Jeff said. In 1982, Mike made the US team as a walk-on, which meant he could train with the squad in Europe but had to pay for all of his expenses.

Mike learned to be creative in how he solicited money. He met with a professional fund-raiser, who showed him how to write letters that from the opening sentence appealed to people's communitarian spirit: "Introducing our new potential Olympian in ski jumping . . ." A few days after mailing letters to local businesses, Mike followed up with phone calls. At first he felt awkward asking for money, but people were happy to help. A majority of the calls resulted in donations of at least five hundred dollars. He didn't realize it at the time, but he was developing skills that he would put to good use years later in his work with investment banks and hedge funds.

Mike placed well enough in his first World Cup competition to earn a berth on the US national team. After that, most of his expenses were picked up by the national ski federation, enabling him to direct all of his focus on cultivating his talent. Future generations of US ski jumpers would not be so fortunate. In 2007, the US Ski and Snowboard Association discontinued its financial support for the sport, forcing every elite-level ski jumper to become his or her own fund-raiser.

In December 1983, in one of the final tune-ups for the 1984 Olympics, Mike, Jeff, and the best ski jumpers in the world gathered in Lake Placid. In a grassroots show of support, a few dozen Norwich residents arranged to take a chartered bus to the competition to cheer on their boys. In an upset, Jeff won the ninety-meter competition to become only the third American to emerge victorious in an international jumping competition. After

Jeff and Mike both realized their dreams by qualifying for the US Olympic team competing in faraway Sarajevo, Yugoslavia, Norwich could not believe its good fortune. How many people never cross paths with a single Olympian? And here the townspeople had two in their midst. This bumper crop was cause for a celebration.

In *An Unlikely Vineyard*, Deirdre Heekin described an atmosphere in which veteran farmers helped their neighbors starting out and rejoiced in their subsequent successes as they would their own. This generosity of spirit spreads like straining roots in quenching soil. To go out of your way for someone you don't know is considered a normal act of kindness in Norwich. But to go out of your way for a neighbor is seen as nothing less than your civic duty. So as Jeff and Mike readied to depart for Yugoslavia, the townspeople sprang into action. Those who had watched the boys grow up got on their telephones to arrange an Olympian send-off. Milt Frye, the principal at Marion Cross at the time, came up with the idea of including the elementary schoolchildren. He thought the three hundred students from kindergarten through sixth grade would gain inspiration from seeing these Olympic athletes up close—athletes who had once squirmed in their seats in the same classrooms, listening to some of the same teachers.

The adults took it from there, planning the send-off as a grand community potluck. They made a banner to hang on Main Street, booked the community Hanover-Norwich Band, created and distributed posters, and wrote and sent out press releases. They compiled a scroll of messages in calligraphy to present to the athletes and made drawings of the boys in action. On the Sunday of the event, they hung American flags along Main Street, served homemade cookies and hot chocolate, and asked people to scream into a resealable plastic bag, which they then closed and presented to Jeff and Mike as a vault of cheers to open when the competition started. Community pride provided the meter in the poem penned by Polly Forcier, a parent who had known Hastings and Holland since they were small children. Years later, she dug up the piece she had written for the boys:

When Jeff was five, a little guy
Out back he piled the snow up high.
He packed the slope and with a whoop
Off that little rise did swoop.
He passed Ford Sayre from A to B
At Sample's Hill began to ski.
He jumped at Leb and at Oak Hill

At night and did his homework still.
Late entered Mike—those Holland genes
With Hastings blood make quite a team.
Jeff's father, Paul, the driving force,
Set the boys upon their course.
Ski jumping has its ups and downs,
Success, hard work and fallen crowns.
But whether they were best or worst
Their courage kept them seeking first.
And now, Godspeed, go far away
Compete for all the U.S.A.
Jump high through Sarajevo's cold
Jeff and Mike—go for gold!

The townspeople felt invested in Mike and Jeff because they had been such an active part of their upbringings. One time, Mike said, he teased a cat on his walk home from school. By the time he strolled through the front door, his mother had already heard about his transgression from a neighbor. "Do you have something to tell me, Mike?" she asked. That is the Norwich that came out in force to send their boys off to Sarajevo, a place most of the people in the town had had to look up on a map. Neither Mike nor Jeff sought attention, and they were both mildly embarrassed by all the fuss being made over them. Didn't their neighbors know the Scandinavians and Eastern Europeans would be the ones likely battling for the gold? But from its recreational league to its Olympians, the town is comfortingly consistent, always emphasizing participation over results.

It took Mike a few years to appreciate the significance of that first Olympic send-off. "We kept hearing for years what an impact it had on some kids who were in the grade school," he said. "They just have vivid memories, and to them, being in this small community made these kids realize, 'Wow, I can go to the Olympics,' and a lot of people did." Tim Tetreault, who was thirteen in February 1984, remembered being inspired by the celebration for Mike and Jeff. Tetreault qualified for his first Olympics in 1992. At his multiathlete send-off, one of the Marion Cross students in attendance was Brett Heyl, who was already showing promise in two sports, kayaking and Alpine skiing. After the children returned to their classrooms, Heyl's teacher used Norwich's Olympic tradition to introduce a probabilities lesson, explaining that the statistics suggested that a current student would grow up to become an Olympian.

"Everyone looked at me like we're done, he's going to be the one," Heyl said. His classmates were right. In 2004, Heyl, then twenty-two, realized his goal when he became the first of Norwich's two homegrown summer Olympians.

In Sarajevo, Jeff was jumping as if in a dream from which he hoped never to wake. During one of the practice sessions, he recorded the longest jump of the day. Once the competition started, he finished fourth on the large hill, missing a medal by less than two meters. If he had graced the medals podium, viewers would have seen the Ford Sayre patch that Jeff had sewn onto his official US Ski Team jacket to acknowledge his roots. His finish was the highest in an Olympics by a US-born jumper. Ask him about his brush with history, and Jeff sounds like the part-time Olympic ski-jumping analyst he would become—detached from the result and armed with facts that frame his accomplishment within a bigger picture. It wasn't that big a deal, he said, because the pool of ski jumpers in the United States was shallow compared to the pool of swimmers or hockey players. And besides, he took pains to point out, his finish wasn't technically the best by an American. He told the story of Anders Haugen, who was born in Norway but emigrated to the

United States with his brother and later finished fourth at the 1924 Olympics. Fifty years later, he was awarded the bronze after a scoring error was discovered in the original results.

Jeff retired after finishing fourth overall on the 1984 World Cup circuit. "I was totally doing it for the love of the sport, and then I moved on," said Jeff, who graduated from Williams College and the Tuck School of Business at Dartmouth and became a senior executive for an automotive supply company. Mike, who had finished outside the top thirty-five in both of his events at the Sarajevo Olympics, continued on in the sport. In 1985, he put together his most memorable season, highlighted by the world record jump in Planica that he replays as part of his annual presentation at Marion Cross. He had visualized that jump so often that it seemed perfectly ordinary to pull it off. Describing the attempt, he said, "It felt like I was lying on my stomach on a glass coffee table, watching a movie projected on a screen underneath the table." Although Mike's jump was nearly flawless, his timing could have been better; if he had set the record at the Olympics, he would have become an overnight sensation. Not that Mike was bothered. A higher profile wouldn't have changed his life much. He still would have returned to Norwich. He still would be volunteering his time to work with youngsters. His life would have followed the same communitarian rhythm that it always has. The only difference, he said, is he might have stayed in the sport longer. He retired in 1989, at age twenty-seven, because he wasn't able to earn enough in ski jumping to cover his expenses.

The year before he retired, Mike participated in his second Olympics. Joining him in Calgary, Alberta, Canada, for the 1988 Games was his younger brother Joe, who had attended—and been inspired by—the 1984 Sarajevo send-off. Jeff's brother Chris also made the US team that year. In the Nordic combined, which consists of jumping and cross-country skiing, Joe finished in the top twenty individual and team events. He also competed at the 1992 Olympics in Albertville, France, along with his baby brother, Jim, and Tim Tetreault, who had Mike to thank for the fact that he was still in the sport. Four years earlier, in his final year of high school, Tim had performed well in regional and national junior Nordic combined competitions. But he headed to the University of Vermont unsure if he should even pack his jumping skis. The discipline was no longer being contested at the collegiate level; the National Collegiate Athletic Association had dropped ski jumping eight years earlier. Wanting to consolidate the snow sports into one championship, the NCAA sacrificed ski jumping to save the Alpine sports.

Tim had calculus and engineering classes to keep him occupied. Would it be a waste of time to continue his Nordic combined career? As he was pondering his future, a postcard arrived out of the blue. It was from Mike, who, during his last competitive tour of Europe, had taken the time to scrawl a few sentences. Tim couldn't recall exactly what he wrote. It was something to the effect of "You're doing great. Keep going." Years later, Tim said, "It was like he had read my mind." Mike's postcard motivated Tim to stick with ski jumping and cross-country skiing. If not for Mike's gesture, Tim almost certainly would not have been on the stage for the 1992 send-off, accepting a bottle of water from Dan & Whit's, the general store, because something in the Norwich water had to account for the town's outsize success.

If Norwich was an Olympic nursery, the Hollands were the tree with the most fruit. John Bower, a longtime US Nordic combined program director, said he had only one criticism of the Hollands' parents: they stopped having children too soon. He joked that the program could use "three or four more" Hollands. I asked Mike's father, Harry, a seventh-generation Vermonter, how he and his wife, parents of five, managed to raise three Olympians. "Maybe some of the success of the boys was because we kept out of the way," he said.

Jim began jumping when he was six but didn't experience much success, he said, until well into his teens. In 1987, Jim, then nineteen, had a horrible crash while jumping and broke his back and wrist. His bones healed, and he decided to stick with the sport, a decision that wasn't easy for his parents to support. But support him they did, and Jim returned to competition with the hard-earned confidence that comes from knowing he had weathered almost the worst the sport could throw at him. Jim went on after the accident to compete in two Olympics. He retired with six national titles. Just as Mike benefited from his friendship with Jeff, so did Jim gain inspiration from being around Mike, whom he credited with setting a positive example. "It just flips a switch in your head," Jim said. "It removes the limitations and makes you reframe what is possible. In many other small towns, going to the Olympics might have seemed out of reach to the average person. But in Norwich it wasn't at all a foreign concept. It was just what people did." Chris

Hastings agreed. He never really thought about the Olympics—it was way down on his list of reasons for jumping.

The Olympics were never built up as a life-defining event by Jeff, Mike, or any of the Norwich Olympians who came after. They treated it as a drawn-out gap year— or in Mike's case, a gap decade. He would need twelve years to complete his engineering degree at the University of Vermont. After years of scheduling classes around the international competition calendar, Mike knew the time to focus on school had come when he signed up for a course taught by a professor who was younger than he was. There was never a question that he eventually would earn his degree. His older sister, Barbara, constantly reminded him that in the United States ski jumping was not, and likely never would be, a lucrative activity. This was before amateurism ceased to be a prerequisite for Olympic consideration. The Olympics are open now to professionals—that is, athletes who are profiting off their sport—but most US Olympians are not getting rich off their success. Fifty percent of the track athletes who rank in the top ten in the United States in their events earn less than fifteen thousand dollars annually. Tim Tetreault, a two-time US champion in Nordic combined with one World Cup podium finish in his career, made thirty thousand dollars in his best year but averaged less than twenty thousand in most years. To add insult to indigence, his state tax return was audited during one of those lean years.

Tim spent several summers working construction as part of a crew assembled by one of his jumping coaches, who recognized that the arrangement provided dual benefits: Tim and the other athletes earned money for college while maintaining their physical conditioning. Whether or not you become an Olympian, education is the real gold medal in Norwich. At the 2014 Sochi Games, freestyle skier Hannah Kearney earned a bronze medal in moguls. In 2015, she won the season-long World Cup title and retired, a decision many in the sport couldn't understand. Why stop when she was performing as well as ever? But no one in Norwich questioned her path. The townspeople recognize that a person's life has seasons, with each transition offering potential for growth. Hannah closed the chapter on her competitive skiing career so she could dive into college textbooks and work toward her undergraduate degree. "If you continue doing something you've done for such a long time, you can't really grow in other ways," Hannah said. She expressed interest in a career in nutrition, motivated by her desire to help people nurture their bodies, minds, and souls.

Another of the Olympians, Chris Hastings, became a chiropractor, but only after working for several years as a coach for the New York Ski Educational Foundation, where he cultivated the careers of jumpers who shared his passion for the sport. He described the work as "the world's best job and the world's worst career" because of the low pay and long hours. "I love coaching," he said. "I love the relationships you build." When Chris realized he probably would never be able to raise a family on his coaching salary, he talked to the parents of his athletes about their jobs. He asked what drew them to their fields and what they liked and didn't like about their work. "By asking questions and talking to people," Chris said, "I was just trying to figure out through them what did I value, what was most important to me moving forward?" One of the people he spoke with was a chiropractor, and their conversation about physical health and healing sparked Chris's interest in the field. He signed up for biology and chemistry classes and pursued his degree.

Growing up in Norwich had taught Chris the value of reaching out to others for help. The well-trod Appalachian Trail runs through Norwich, and the residents are generous in providing assistance—be it a meal, bed, shower, or ride—to hikers who stumble into their town. The town's pride of place manifests itself in other ways. For years one resident voluntarily replaced bags for dog waste in the Milton Frye Nature Area, where people walk their pets—and where their children roam—and emptied the trash receptacles where those bags were deposited. The athletes of Norwich learn from the example of people like Sig Evensen, a longtime ski jumper and international judge who could be found on event days packing the snow on the landing, raking the track, or fixing someone's cracked ski. "He'd go to all the competitions and work his ass off to make sure all the jumps were in perfect shape," Chris said of Sig, who died of cancer in 1999. "And he always had a kind word for everyone."

Sig made an impression on the Hastings and Holland brothers, who all give freely of their time and expertise. They've coached for the Ford Sayre program that gave them their start. And during the New Hampshire high school ski-jumping season, it is not unusual on a meet day to find Chris announcing, Jeff serving as a judge, and Mike smoothing the snow at the bottom of the landing hill after wipeouts—after they've all chipped in to pack the jump. They've taken the resources they received from Norwich as youngsters and poured them back into the community. To a man, they insist their labor of love is less about paying off a debt than tapping into fond memories and imparting life lessons. After a competition in the winter of 2017, Mike told the jumpers the sport was shaping their lives in ways they probably wouldn't be able to appreciate until much later. No matter whether they won or lost, they were learning to confront difficult tasks and take risks while developing the confidence that comes from mastering a challenging skill. "At a very young age you are learning an approach to life that only a tiny fraction of the population ever learns," he said.

None of the jumpers got wealthy off the sport—far from it—and yet they express appreciation for all the ways the sport continues to enrich their lives. As Jeff noted after raking the landing area early on one of the first nights of the season, "The sport continues to give me far more than I could ever repay." Gratitude was soldered into the ski-jumping contraption that Mike designed and built. His brother Jim donated the seed money to fund the production of several of the devices, each of which costs roughly three thousand dollars to build. Mike sells them to US ski clubs for $495 and donates the money to the national federation for ski jumping and Nordic combined. He has the clubs pay for the machines so that they'll value them more. It is sound logic, as any teenager who had to work to buy his or her first car can surely attest. It's impossible to put a price on the value of all these gestures. I talked to a mother with three young children who told me that the opportunity to learn from Olympians is an exquisite gift. It coaxes the town's youth outside on days when the weather is better suited for playing video games or watching television. Another mother told me that her son believed that he, too, could make it to the Olympics one day because Jeff, Mike, and the others have shown him that Olympians aren't superheroes. They shop at Dan & Whit's and stroll along Main Street. The town could erect bronze statues to honor its distinguished residents, but what would be the point? Better to have them walking around, tangible testaments to the Norwich way.

Norwich does maintain a shrine to its Olympians in Tracy Hall, the town's nerve center, but in an inconspicuous place: on a wall alongside stairs leading to the second-floor office of the recreation director. Framed photographs of Olympians climb the wall, sharing space with an inexpensive wooden plaque with each Olympian's name engraved on a gold plate: the Alpine skiers

Betsy Snite and Felix McGrath; the jumpers Jeff and Chris Hastings and Mike and Jim Holland; the Nordic combined specialists Joe Holland and Tim Tetreault; the kayaker Brett Heyl; the freestyle skier Hannah Kearney; and the runner Andrew Wheating. Several more plates are blank, including one with a message on a piece of paper the size of a gum wrapper taped to it. "Your name here," the message reads. "Keep the Norwich Olympic tradition going. Train Hard, Dream Big and Amazing Things Can Happen."

The Olympic send-off that Norwich treated as a one-off back in 1984 has become a ritual—with Olympians past, present, and future intertwined like the five Olympic rings. Hannah played in the band when Tim Tetreault was feted. Brook Leigh was a flag bearer at one of Hannah's send-offs; in 2015 his US freestyle national championship debut was her swan song. Jeff and Mike have become the regular emcees of these celebrations, which seems only fitting, since they inspired the first. They emphasize that the stage may be bigger, but the goal at the Olympics should be the same: to have fun and make memories. Instead of weighing down the departing athletes with expectations, they present them with gag gifts. The 800-meter runner Andrew Wheating received two cans of baked beans before the 2008 Summer Games in Beijing, the better to clear a row of seats for his added comfort during the long flight. Everybody gets a plastic bag sealed with cheers. At Hannah's third and final send-off, in 2014, Mike reminded the grade schoolers in the audience that they could grow up to be the next Norwich Olympians. Ever the champion for his sport, he announced that the next ski-jumping practice was the following evening. "Bring your Alpine skis, bring your parents, boots, and helmets," he said.

His presentation at Marion Cross in front of some of the same students the following year earned him several enthusiastic jumpers. Alas, the weather didn't cooperate. All the snow melted soon thereafter, ending the ski season before it had taken flight. Mike was unfazed. He summoned the can-do spirit that has helped him prosper as an athlete and a person and came up with a plan. By the next winter, he had acquired snowmaking equipment. In Norwich, where there's a will, there's an Olympian leading the way.

3

HOSANNAS FOR HANNAH

Lesson: *Grounded by Unconditional Support*

The early settlers in Norwich planted seeds from the tastiest apples but were often confounded when the resultant trees produced fruit that was not as good as the original. Through trial and error, they discovered they could obtain the desired results by taking cuttings from the trees with the best apples and grafting them onto healthy root stock. In modern-day Norwich, the moguls skier Hannah Kearney was like the seeds of those apples. She thrived when attached to the community, which balanced her tart self-critiques and cushioned her from bruising.

Hannah's roots in Norwich run as deep as those of its other homegrown Olympians. She was born at the Dartmouth-Hitchcock Medical Center in Lebanon, New Hampshire, and brought home to a house that sits along a two-lane asphalt road five miles from the Norwich town center—an easy training jog for her. She had the drive and the desire to succeed, but without Norwich's support, both financial and emotional, her Olympic dreams might have withered. Hannah was one of those highly competitive athletes—the kind of compulsively motivated personality classically associated with champions—that occasionally take root in the town. But instead of nurturing that obsession, Norwich does the opposite. It prunes back the pressure and provides the soft landing needed for the inevitable failures. Hannah could have become another victim of maladaptive perfectionism. Instead she is a happy, seemingly well-adjusted adult, because Norwich taught her to love herself in spite of her inner magistrate, who is always judging her actions.

The town's ethos echoes the philosophy set forth in the late nineteenth century by the Frenchman Pierre de Coubertin, the founder of the modern Olympics. In reviving the ancient Games in 1896, he said the most important thing was not winning but taking part, just as the essential thing in life was not conquering but fighting well. That sums up the approach in Norwich, where sports are a means of self-expression, a vehicle to sharpen one's life skills, and an integral part of a healthy routine.

Hannah's parents, Jill and Tom, met as students at Montreal's McGill University, where Tom was a receiver on the football team. They were athletic, outdoorsy types, drawn to Norwich by the hiking trails and ski runs carved out of the state's Green Mountains. They followed Tom's brother, Pat, who was working for a contractor in nearby Lyme, New Hampshire. Tom was employed by another contractor before he and Pat struck out on their own in the 1980s. Hannah's mother taught physical education at Hanover High before settling into a position as Norwich's recreation director, a job she has held for more than twenty years. Hannah's father eventually took over the business he and his brother had started. Hannah was born on February 26, 1986. She was Jill and Tom's first child, followed twenty-three months later by her brother, Denny. Her parents brought her home to a rustic wood-framed structure set on three and a half acres bordered by a tree-lined gully. It is near the Union Village Dam, operated by the Army Corps of Engineers.

The family often held picnics there. It was an idyllic place to raise children, with an abundance of open space to explore.

Her parents had bought the house in foreclosure in the early 1980s for twenty-six thousand dollars. They drained their savings to make the purchase, and then Tom stripped the house to its bones. He spent the next ten years meticulously rebuilding it. He toiled nights and weekends to finish the three-story dwelling, which has hardwood floors throughout, a wood-burning stove, and large windows framing the pine, birch, and maple trees outside. Hannah and her brother had their own rooms on the second floor, but Hannah gradually took over the third-floor attic, where she nested like a mouse between walls adorned with glittery stars. Homes in the area on comparable tracts of land now sell for prices in excess of half a million dollars, but Hannah cannot imagine selling the property. It is her sanctum. Her brother's wedding took place on the grounds in 2016, and her father continues to run his construction company out of two barns on the land.

The family's property, where their visitors included deer, wild turkeys, foxes, groundhogs, and the occasional moose, was the perfect playground for the active, woodsy family. Hannah's athleticism revealed itself early. At five months, she could stand on the palm of her mother's hand like a gymnast on a balance beam. Encouraged by her motor skills, her parents introduced Hannah to skiing when she was two years old. Her earliest memory of being on the snow was skiing in between her mother's legs, first on the gently sloping hills on the family's property and then at the Dartmouth Skiway, a few miles away in Lyme, New Hampshire. She quickly advanced to skiing while secured in a horse halter while her mother, a riding enthusiast, skied behind her. Jill reined her in only if Hannah got going too fast.

Hannah followed a well-worn path for the children of Norwich, enrolling at the age of six in the program at Dartmouth Skiway, which offered instruction at a minimal cost. The Ford Sayre ski school was where all the Norwich Olympians, including the town's first, Betsy Snite, got their starts. By the time Hannah joined in the second grade there was also instruction in upright aerials, moguls, and acro skiing, ballet performed on snow. In the application, Hannah's parents were asked to check the word that best described their child's skiing style. The choices were "cautious," "average," and "aggressive." They marked the "aggressive" box.

The Ford Sayre program fostered family participation by using parent volunteers as teachers—they received free training from certified ski instructors, many of whom had ties to the Dartmouth program. The idea was to introduce skiing as an activity that families could enjoy together. Hannah's family embraced the Ford Sayre ethos, with her mother giving freely of her time on the slopes. For them, skiing was a family bonding exercise, one that encouraged conversation during the chairlift rides up the mountain and competition during the bumpy rides down. As a child, Hannah said, she saw no other reason for her involvement in the sport. As she would later say, skiing was a way to enjoy both winter and her family. This attitude jibed with the town's collective belief that hibernation is best left to the bears. Norwich aims to establish outdoor activities as a winter habit early on by letting students at the single elementary school in town, Marion Cross, out of classes early every Wednesday so they can travel by bus or carpool to the Dartmouth Skiway for a nominal cost. Hannah so looked forward to these midweek outings that she would wear her ski clothes to school so she didn't have to waste time changing. That way she was able to squeeze in an extra run or two.

Hannah had always been athletic and an outdoors enthusiast, but she had a fastidious side. As a toddler, she lined up her toys as if she were a soldier preparing for a barracks inspection. Her mother was puzzled by this attention to detail. Where did she acquire this need for order? It was not, she said with a twinkle in her eye, an inherited trait. To her parents' surprise, the little girl who was careful about coloring inside the lines, who assiduously followed instructions, enjoyed skiing outside the course boundaries. The mounds of snow off to the side of the groomed trails appealed to Hannah more than the runs. Her personality underwent a transformation when she was on skis or on the soccer pitch. The introverted child morphed into a cutthroat competitor.

At the age of nine, Hannah joined the freestyle ski program at Waterville Valley, New Hampshire, about an hour's drive from Norwich, and jumped headlong into United States Ski and Snowboard Association–sanctioned competitions. She didn't finish among the leaders at first, but she didn't care. Hannah loved being outdoors and having an outlet for her competitiveness. Most of all, given her meticulous nature, she liked that she could chart her improvement. Every time she traipsed to her mother's second-floor office at Tracy Hall, Hannah received an inspiring reminder of where her progress could eventually lead. As she climbed the staircase, she would tap the photos on the wall of the athletes from the town who competed in the Olympics. Hannah didn't exactly understand what the Olympics were, but her goal of adding her own photo to Norwich's wall of fame took shape in 1998 when she played the trumpet in the band that performed "The Star-Spangled Banner" at a send-off ceremony for Tim Tetreault before his third Olympics. Norwich had been holding Olympic send-offs since before Hannah was born, but this was the first one that she remembered. The pomp and pageantry made an indelible impression on her sixth-grade self, as did emcee Mike Holland's speech that any of the schoolkids could one day have their own Olympic send-off.

But as much as she loved skiing, Hannah could not imagine growing up with it as her sole focus. She rode horses, ran track, and was an all-state soccer player in high school, all while earning straight As. For a long time, Hannah dreamed of skiing in the Winter Olympics and competing in track in the Summer Games, taking the Norwich philosophy of changing sports with the seasons to its extreme, as was her nature. Her high school soccer coach said she was good enough to play the sport in college, but as Hannah's love of freestyle skiing swelled, she embraced soccer and track as activities that gave her much-needed mental breaks from skiing while allowing her to maintain her cardiovascular conditioning.

Though Hannah proved adept at whatever she tried, her participation wasn't contingent on her proficiency. The recreation department her mother oversees offers no-cut leagues in a variety of sports, from fencing to soccer. Everybody is afforded the chance to play, and on the rare occasion when a coach, usually in his or her first year, strays from that philosophy, Jill will sit down with the offender to reinforce the league priorities. These recreational teams offered Hannah her first exposure to the people whose nonjudgmental acceptance would counterbalance her perfectionism. Through the leagues, Hannah got the chance to know girls who were neither as competitive nor as athletically oriented as herself. Through the years they would become some of her dearest friends. "It takes me a long time to warm up to people," Hannah said. "I don't have time to waste my bubbliness on everyone. The no-cut rules allowed me six years to make friends." Long after Hannah aged out of the recreational leagues, the relationships she made in them thrived. Her peers, who grew up to become a forester, nurse, entrepreneur, market manager, and radio show host, would keep Hannah connected to a world where no one cared how long it took her to race down a mountain. Before she left on a long trip, her school friends would present her with greeting cards filled with messages and signatures so that she could carry pieces of them with her.

Of all the sports she played, skiing was the best fit for her personality. It appealed to her solitary nature, and she liked that once her skis were pointed toward the bottom of a mountain, there was no turning back. From a young age, Hannah showed a fierce determination to finish whatever she started. Jeff Hastings described Hannah as "the most aggressive, driven athlete" he had ever been around. Like Betsy Snite on skis before her, Hannah's no-holds-barred approach on the soccer pitch drew comparisons to the boys. "There was talk about her playing high school soccer like no other guy ever had before at Hanover High," Jeff said.

Hannah's teachers at Marion Cross expressed concern to her parents that she was overly serious for someone so young, and did their best to slacken the pressure when she got wound up. In the third grade, Hannah walked into class on the first day and burst into tears because she had to share a table with other students.

She had anticipated having her own desk. The next year, her gym teacher stepped in and stopped her from doing more sit-ups than necessary during the President's Council on Fitness, Sports & Nutrition tests. She was concerned that Hannah had taken the instruction "Do as many as you can" and processed it as "Do more than anybody no matter what" and was in danger of pulling a muscle from overexertion. "I remember an eighth-grade teacher saying, 'Hannah needs to lighten up and relax,'" Hannah said. "But it's hard to change your personality."

Hannah's competitive drive was not something her father could rewire like an electrical panel in the wall of a building. He remembered taking his children to the playground at Huntley Meadow. Hannah would quickly tire of playing on the swings, and when that happened, she'd coax her brother into a footrace. Or they'd create an obstacle course and take turns completing it as fast as they could. Hannah insisted that her father clock them so she could see how she measured up to her brother or to track her own improvement—because of course she kept track of her times. It didn't dawn on her until years later that her behavior was not the norm in Norwich. On a rare free afternoon after Hannah had graduated from high school, she met up at Huntley Meadow with a group of classmates for a barbecue. Some of the kids were headed to Ivy League schools, but for all their ambition, nobody could relate to the story Hannah regaled them with of running timed races against her brother in the very spot on which they sat. Her friends fell silent until one spoke up and said the story shed a klieg light on her personality. If she was that driven, that competitive, as a child, no wonder she had grown into an intense teenager who was so tough on herself.

Hannah's intensity did help her become a world-class competitor. The repetition of movements, in search of technical precision if not perfection, fed her obsessive nature. She kept meticulous training logs, which showed that by the end of her career she had suited up 425 times and climbed 398,475 stairs in her ski boots in order to execute 6,325 jumps, honing her helicopter turns and backflips until these unnatural movements became second nature. Her mother was among those who marveled at her commitment. "I kept thinking, 'Where's the limit?'" she said.

Hannah did not feel at ease performing some of the more advanced tricks. She had already become a US national team member when the rules she had grown up with suddenly changed: inversions were added to her sport. She had little enthusiasm for backflips, but she learned to do them for the same reason someone with a dislike of root vegetables pinches her nose and eats the beets on her plate. She knew it would benefit her in the long run.

There is a price to be paid for swallowing fear day after day, for turning one's focus inward to execute the same tasks over and over. Hannah threw herself into the air even on days when she was so sick she was throwing up. She won competitions when she was feverish, retreating between runs to the lodge of the resort where the race was taking place and crawling into the fetal position right on the lobby floor. As with other elite athletes, Hannah risked sacrificing the qualities that made her human in pursuit of the goal of performing like a machine. Hannah's consistency made it seem like she was more metronome than mortal. She graced the medals podium in 60 percent of her races on the freestyle international circuit and posted forty-six World Cup victories. Between January 2011 and February 2012, she won sixteen consecutive World Cup races. But on occasion she faltered, and when that happened she was thankful for the friends and neighbors who were unfailingly there for her.

Hannah's career likely would have been neither as

long nor as illustrious if not for the generosity of her neighbors, because for all her ability in negotiating bumps on the slopes, the expense of the sport presented a more difficult obstacle for Hannah to navigate. At the time that she qualified for her first junior US championships at age thirteen, her family lacked the disposable income to take annual trips to Europe or buy new skis every year like her friends whose parents were doctors or tenured professors at Dartmouth. She made do with clothing and equipment that she found at consignment shops or acquired from neighbors. She was fortunate to grow up in a place quick to help those in need.

I saw this myself, again and again. I was standing in the front office of the elementary school when a boy approached the secretary to ask about a piece of pizza, that day's offering for students who qualified for the free-lunch program. He had not received his, and he was hungry. The secretary scrambled to produce a makeshift lunch of applesauce, a packet of peanut butter crackers, and a piece of fruit. The father of the Olympian Brett Heyl attended Marion Cross in the 1960s, when half the student body was the offspring of farmers. Those days are gone. Today the school is populated by children of college-educated parents with shallower roots in Norwich, prosperous families drawn to the town because of its excellent public schools. Yet Hannah and others insist that the town's growing affluence does not mean that the children from less well-off families are left behind. "You don't find people using the town's resources but not giving back," Hannah said. At her recreation office, Hannah's mother routinely fields calls from residents offering to pay the recreation-league fees for children in need. Like the ski school founder Ford Sayre in the 1930s, people still want to remove any obstacles to participation.

When Hannah was ready to broaden her scope from local and regional competitions to national events, her parents sat her down and explained that they could not afford to send her to races anywhere that required airplane flights and hotel stays. If she wanted to continue, she was going to have to find sponsors. They left her to figure out the details. Years later, Hannah's mother would read a novel in which parents take out a second mortgage to finance the Olympic aspirations of their gymnast daughter. I've known parents who have gone to those lengths, but Jill considered the work of fiction far-fetched. She couldn't imagine risking the family's financial well-being to fund a child's sports dreams. "Who would do that?" she said.

Hannah's parents encouraged her to compose a résumé that listed her skiing accomplishments and her grades, which she distributed all over town. Hannah also included business cards she had crafted for the occasion, that listed sports as her favorite activity. Through her efforts, she secured sponsorship from a local car dealership, which helped defray her expenses. But money remained tight. Then a casual conversation between Hannah's mother and a member of the Norwich Recreation Council led to a phone call from the council member's father, a self-made millionaire who wanted to help. He would provide funds for Hannah's skiing and asked for only two things in return: a copy of her grades every term and a detailed budget of how she spent the money. The man's munificence and the terms of his generosity, were consistent with the town's approach of nurturing the whole child and not just the athlete (or the musician or the student). Years later, Hannah expressed gratitude for the man's gift of money—and perspective. "It was all about my report cards, not my ski results," she said, "and in being that way he was sending the message that investing in your brain is a little more long-term than investing in freestyle skiing." Hannah never met her benefactor, but his presence in her life loomed large. His financial aid kept her in the sport until she became a member of the US Ski Team, at which point the national sports federation paid most of her expenses. Sponsorships with equipment manufacturers and clothing companies helped cover the rest of her costs—and allowed her to save money for college.

Without the sponsorships, Hannah estimated that she would have had to scrape together an extra fifty thousand dollars a year—the costs for coaching and training and travel not covered by the ski federation—to continue to compete at a world-class level. It helped that Hannah was naturally frugal. In the lead-up to her second Olympics, she discontinued the cable television service at her house, having reasoned that between her out-of-town training trips and the competitive season in Europe, she wasn't around enough to justify the costs. By then her parents had divorced and moved out. Both would remarry and move into new residences. For a yo-yoing Hannah and Denny, a professional hockey player in Europe, the house was the place they kept returning to as their careers unspooled all over the world.

Hannah considered herself fortunate that Norwich was a three-hour drive from the US Olympic Training Center in Lake Placid, New York, which had facilities—including a sports science laboratory and jumping complex—found in only a few other places in the country. After high school, Hannah faithfully spent five months a year at Lake Placid, twice an Olympic host, because the free room and board she received helped defray costs. She was a familiar presence in the summers, practicing new aerial tricks at the Olympic Jumping Complex.

In 2002, the United States hosted the Winter Games for the first time since Lake Placid in 1980. They took place in Salt Lake City, Utah, which, with its state-of-the-art facilities, then became the new base for US winter sports. Hannah could have moved semipermanently to Salt Lake, and she would in fact take up temporary residence there to attend college after her skiing career was over. But as long as she was competing, she leaned on Norwich for the nurturing that, as the runner Andrew Wheating would later discover, can be hard to find in the performance-oriented professional sports culture.

In 2006, Hannah competed in her first Olympics. She was nineteen years old and two years out of high school. She traveled to the Winter Games in Turin, Italy, with great expectations. The previous year she had become the first American to win the moguls title at the World Championships, beating essentially the same competition that she would face at the Olympics. If she had beaten all the skiers the year before, who was going to stand between her and a gold medal? Hannah had entered races as the favorite before, but never with the world watching. Reporters who couldn't locate Norwich on a map highlighted her in their stories. She felt pressure to perform, not simply to make her family proud but to do right by Norwich and reflect well on America. That's a lot to shoulder, and in her first run, Hannah faltered. Racing as she always did with her pigtails squirting out of her helmet, she failed to stick the landing on her opening jump, a helicopter 360, and her off-balance landing caused her to teeter through her remaining turns. In her event, competitors are judged on turns, jumps, and speed, and Hannah came up short in all three areas. She finished twenty-second, two spots shy of advancing to the final and staying alive for a medal.

Hannah was devastated. She couldn't help but think of everyone back in Norwich, and the send-off fit for a champion. On a frigid January morning, shortly before she left for Italy, several hundred people had braved the cold to show their support. The three-hundred-member Marion Cross student body was there, and so was a reporter from the local newspaper, who noted in his story that children held up handmade signs that read "Hannah Hustles" and

"Ms. Moxie Moguls." Mike Holland presented Hannah with a bottle of Norwich tap water drawn from the bathroom sink at Dan & Whit's and a plastic sandwich bag that was sealed after the students had shouted encouragement into it. All that love that she had carried in that plastic bag—and in her heart—she had repaid with a poor performance. She felt as if she had embarrassed Norwich. That was the word she used: *embarrassed*. Meeting with reporters afterward, her eyes filled with tears. She was led away, sobbing, by a US skiing official.

Hannah returned home feeling like a snow angel whose wings had been clipped. She was unprepared for the reception she received. When she ducked into Dan & Whit's for staples like eggs, milk, and bread, her fellow shoppers stopped her in the narrow aisles to say how proud they were of her for representing Norwich on the world stage. Everywhere she went, people were positive. They sounded genuinely excited that she had taken part in the Olympics. No one framed her Olympic debut as a failure. No one averted their gazes when they saw her approaching. "No one said, 'Oh, we're so sorry,'" Hannah marveled. "I was nineteen years old and had gone to the Olympics. People acted like that was fantastic."

As a result, she was able to move past her defeat in

a matter of weeks. Ten years later, I described Hannah's 2006 homecoming to a champion swimmer, whose eyes grew large. After a summer in which she struggled in the water, she returned home, she said, and was shopping when she stopped to converse with a man whose daughter had once been a rival. The man said his family was praying that she would be able to turn her results around, and quickly, since the Rio de Janeiro Olympics were just months off. With support like that, who needs censure? Hannah couldn't conceive of that conversation happening in Norwich, where the townspeople, having watched her grow up, could read her moods as well as they could their own children's.

The nonjudgmental support began, but did not end, with her parents, whose greatest contribution to their children's sports careers was simply showing up. Tom and Jill provided nurturing and left the rest to Hannah and Denny, who started his pro hockey career in the lower-tier leagues in the United States and then found his niche in Europe. A six-foot-one forward, Denny played at Yale before embarking on his adventure abroad, which has included stops in Germany, France, Norway, Sweden, and Italy. He has succeeded with a decidedly more laid-back personality than Hannah, who once bet Denny a hundred dollars that he wouldn't drop his gloves and fight an opponent, a former college nemesis, during an American Hockey League game his first year as a pro. To Hannah's delight, he did drop his hockey gloves and skirmish with the player. As soon as she saw him after the game, Hannah theatrically peeled five twenty-dollar bills from her wallet and paid off her wager.

Norwich's support carried Hannah to glory four years later. At the 2010 Vancouver Olympics, she was again the favorite. On the day of her race, she crouched in the gatehouse and experienced a sense of peace that had eluded her in Italy. Her fate would be decided in less than a minute, but unlike in 2006, she knew the results wouldn't define her. She had already failed on the biggest stage, and the people of Norwich had been no less proud of her. She felt as if she had nothing to lose, and that freed her to win.

A veil of fog hung over Cypress Mountain, site of the women's moguls final. Hannah led after the first run, which meant she was the final competitor down the knobby, two-jumps course. She set her skis in the starting gate and soaked in the scene. On a clear day, she would have had a breathtaking view of the Vancouver skyline and the harbor. The dreary conditions were less than ideal, but they suited her beautifully. She noted the patches of bare muddy earth on either side of the run and the slick, granular surface, so similar to the conditions in which she grew up skiing at New Hampshire's Waterville Valley resort. She felt at home, and she skied like it, performing a flawless straight back layout with a cross on her first jump and a helicopter 360 on the second to secure the gold. It was the first American victory in Vancouver and the first ever for Norwich, surpassing the silver won by Alpine skier Betsy Snite in 1960. When she accepted her gold during the medals ceremony, Hannah had another medal, shaped like the state of Vermont and made of silver, hidden under her shirt, close to her heart.

Back in Norwich, the townspeople decided a celebration was in order. They huddled at Dan & Whit's or logged on to the community message board from home to plan a parade. Dan Fraser, of Dan & Whit's, designed a bumper sticker to express Norwich's pride: "Hannah Kearney, 2010 Olympic Gold Medalist in Freestyle Skiing." At the bottom, in almost indecipherably small type, he included the store's name and address. Fraser made the bumper stickers available for a dollar apiece and quickly sold out. He presented Kearney with a hundred-dollar check, the amount of the proceeds, which she donated to the Norwich Public Library, where she had checked out books every week as a youngster. She asked the children's librarian, Beth Reynolds, to use the money for titles of interest to young girls. Reynolds bought books on cold-weather sports and from the American Girl nonfiction series. When Hannah's mother found out, she felt prouder than when Hannah won the gold medal. She would never broadcast what her daughter had done, but she hoped other parents and their kids heard about the gesture. "Because you want that community mentality passed on," she said.

Several Norwich youngsters dressed up, pigtails and all, as Hannah for Halloween. Beyond the town, her renown grew. She threw out the ceremonial first pitch at a Boston Red Sox game, but her gold medal did not set her up for life. For three years after her 2010 victory, Hannah made more than a quarter of a million dollars annually through her endorsements and performance bonuses. But as she prepared to defend her Olympic title in 2014, she noticed that the endorsement opportunities were drying up. Twelve events were added to the program for the Sochi Olympics, and the pond of athletes available to companies fishing for brand ambassadors had become overstocked. As a result, fewer lines were being cast in her direction. It didn't matter to Hannah, who had never gotten into the sport to get rich or even to eke out a sustainable living long-term. But she could not ignore that the next generation of women who rose to challenge her supremacy included a few hypnotized by the dollar signs dangled before them by parents and coaches. Her rivals included burned-out gymnasts and divers who switched to freestyle skiing because they viewed it as another track to the Olympics. She saw ten-year-olds forgoing regular school for correspondence courses in the quest to become Olympic champions. She watched preteens leave their homes for boarding schools so they could train all day, seven days a week. She never felt more fortunate to be a child of Norwich than in 2014 in Sochi, Russia, when she watched a US teammate dissolve into tears because she was afraid to call her parents back home after failing to medal in her event.

Hannah had decided that the Sochi Games would be her last Olympics. She was eager to turn her focus to obtaining her degree. She had started college, using her skiing earnings to pay for classes at Dartmouth in the springs when she was home, but she was twenty-seven years old and still many units shy of finishing. Hannah's plan was to finish her schooling at Salt Lake City's West-minster College, which offered scholarships to US national ski team members. She had continued to dominate her event in the years after her gold-medal performance in Vancouver, and the opportunity to go out on top, so rare among athletes, greatly appealed to her. She wanted to avoid sticking with her sport too long and becoming someone whose career ended in a slow fade. Having hiked the hills around her home from the time she could walk, Hannah was aware that the descent could be more treacherous than the ascent.

During one stretch in the lead-up to Sochi, Hannah strung together sixteen consecutive victories. She wasn't even aware of it. She almost took a year off in the middle of the streak to make headway on her college degree. In a news report before the Sochi Games, Hannah was described as "the closest thing there is to a sure thing on snow." But as she knew only too well, in Olympic sports nothing is scripted; no result is preordained. The pressure to produce one's best performance once every four years when the world is watching is intense. The body, the mind, and Mother Nature all have to be in sync. Athletes can spend three years winning consistently only to arrive at the Olympics and get thrown off by a sinus infection, food poisoning, or unexpected weather. The strain on Hannah was exacerbated by the fact that she was chasing history. She had the chance to become the first woman to win back-to-back moguls titles at the Olympics. The pressure prevented Hannah from performing at her best in Sochi. In each of her runs, she struggled on the same bump. On her last run, she landed awkwardly after her opening jump, and her left ski splayed. She had to summon all her years of experience to remain upright. Hannah's final jump of that run, which included a challenging grab of her ski, was not enough to vault her past the up-and-coming Canadian sisters Justine and Chloe Dufour-Lapointe. Hannah was inconsolable. She replayed her mistake over and over. She cried most of the night.

If she had performed a flawless routine and lost, it would have been easier to accept. But to ski less than her best when it most mattered was devastating. After she got back to her room in the athletes' village, Hannah tweeted a message that reflected her black mood: "Bronze feels a lot like a broken heart." Back in Norwich, townspeople saw the post and knew what they had to do. Dan Fraser reached out to townsfolk about organizing a homecoming celebration for Hannah. Who cared if it wasn't a victory parade? It was worth recognizing the end of her remarkable Olympic career.

Molly Riordan, who had three children under the age of ten and was pregnant with her fourth, had watched the Olympics and been heartbroken to see Hannah's tears. She wanted her to know that nobody was disappointed. To the contrary, Riordan found much to admire in how Hannah had owned up to her failure to defend her Olympic title. Riordan sewed banners that she then auctioned off for charitable causes. She described it as her "Zen activity." She agreed to make the banner for the homecoming. It took ten hours, spread out over five nights, and all the felt material she had in her house, to complete the four-by-five-foot project. It was the largest banner she had ever attempted, but Riordan had a lot to convey to Hannah in the space. Riordan's firstborn, a son, was a ten-year-old ski racer at the time. He had had his photograph taken with Hannah and wanted to help make her feel better. So he and his siblings worked with their mother to arrange the letters on the material. Against a white background, Riordan carefully cut out letters from red, white, and blue felt pieces to read,

Hannah Kearney Norwich's Hero
2-Time Olympic Medalist
Making Us Proud the World Over.

On the day of the parade, Hannah rode into town behind fire truck escorts. The banner, hung from the gazebo on the town green, caught her eye. She gazed at it for several seconds, taking note of the painstaking craftsmanship, and tears formed in the corners of her eyes. That signage, like Hannah's banner career, underscored the same lesson: there is beauty in sticking with something long after others would have given up. Dan Fraser delivered a speech. Though he referred to notes, he spoke from the heart when he said, "We are so proud of you for doing more than any of us could ever have imagined possible." The microphone burbled with static, but his message was crystal clear. Watching her compete in three Olympics, Fraser added, provided a sense of accomplishment for the whole town. "You have no idea what you have given us," he said, "especially these youngsters here. Now more than ever you have provided everyone with a role model to admire." Fraser concluded by saying that Kearney's Olympic success was not the end: "You have shown you have what it takes to succeed at anything you set your mind to. Go out and conquer your next challenge."

I first met Hannah eight months after that homecoming parade. We had lunch with her mother at the

Norwich Inn, where Hannah splurged on zucchini fries, one of her favorite indulgences. Blue placards heralding her Olympic participation still hung in the windows of the local bank and a real-estate office. Hannah's blond hair, which she gathered in double braids when she competed, hung loosely on her shoulders. She is listed as five foot six and 152 pounds, but she looked doll-like in person, her piston-like legs hidden beneath a flannel skirt. Hannah's eyes welled when she recalled the reception she received upon her return from Sochi. Once again the town had granted her permission to forgive herself for being fully human, which is to say, imperfect. "Norwich finds the right balance of raising you to have high expectations for your life and for your future, but not expecting, demanding, a specific kind of success," she said.

One of the people in the audience during her Sochi homecoming was Wendy Thompson, who had taught Hannah in the third and fourth grades at Marion Cross. Mrs. T., as she is affectionately known to her students, had been the one to calm Hannah when she became hysterical at not having her own big-girl desk, and had marveled at the precision of Hannah's cursive writing and her determination to master her multiplication tables. After the ceremony, Thompson approached Hannah and told her she had a gift for her at the school. Hannah followed Thompson back to her classroom, where a stanza from a Lewis Carroll poem greets all at the door. "'The time has come,' the Walrus said, 'To talk of many things: Of shoes and ships and sealing wax, of cabbages and kings. And why the sea is boiling hot and whether pigs have wings.'" Hannah waited while Thompson rummaged through a pile on her desk. As part of a "Westward Movement" project during the class's study of the Oregon Trail, Hannah had cross-stitched a little house with "Home Sweet Home" above it with a precision that had floored Thompson. After years of holding on to the project for safekeeping, the teacher decided it was the ideal time to open Hannah's eyes to her own talents. She presented the needlepoint to Hannah, who smiled in recognition. Recounting the story years later, she laughed. Other than a parent, who holds on to a third grader's project for twenty years? Only in Norwich, where the town treats every child as its own.

4

SETTING HIS OWN PACE

Lesson: *Let Nature Run Its Course*

Jeff Johnson could not believe he had been coaxed out of hibernation for this. His natural inclination was to hole up in the old barn in Lebanon, New Hampshire, that he had converted into a cavernous but cozy retreat, on land that he shared with wild turkeys and deer and chipmunks. Johnson spent so much time alone with the undomesticated creatures that he gave them congenial names: Doug for a friendly woodchuck; Ernie for a chipmunk. Jeff felt more of a kinship with the wildlife that wanted only to be fed than the civilized people with their appetites and agendas. But Jeff had been a decent college miler once, as well as Nike's first full-time employee. A friend's tall tale was what had lured him out of his man barn and into the dingy light of the Dartmouth College indoor track, where Jeff was standing with a stopwatch around his neck and tenebrous thoughts forming in his mind as Andrew Wheating loped past him.

From what he could see, Andrew should have stuck with soccer. "Hopeless, just hopeless," Jeff muttered to himself as Andrew took his first lap around Leverone Field House's six-lane, two-hundred-meter track. He seemed like a nice, earnest young man, but what fool takes up competitive track as a senior in high school and expects his career to go anywhere but in circles? Jeff and Andrew, who had just met, were the only people in the hangar-like structure with arched ceilings and low lighting. The building, situated across the Connecticut River from Norwich, where Andrew lived with his parents and two younger siblings, was designed by an Italian engineer and architect, Pier Luigi Nervi, whose handiwork included a few of the venues for the 1960 Summer Olympics in Rome. Jeff, who had run against a couple of the stars of those Games while an undergraduate at Stanford, was long retired from Nike. He had agreed to evaluate Andrew's running potential as a favor to a coach and administrator at Kimball Union Academy, the coed, 345-student private high school in New Hampshire that Andrew attended as a day student.

Andrew's relaxed strides called to mind a dog ambling back to the doorstep after baring its teeth at the mail deliverer. If anybody had wandered in from the cold, they might have taken one look at his pale, lanky six-foot-six frame and assumed, not unreasonably, that he was a basketball player working to improve his conditioning under the watchful gaze of his snowy-haired coach. Youngsters with Andrew's build are typically steered into basketball because they possess the one strength that can't be taught: size. Andrew did spend three seasons on the junior varsity basketball team at Kimball Union, but mostly because his school required each student to participate in two athletic activities, the better to strengthen their bodies, stretch their comfort zones, and foster teamwork. His play under the basket belied the belief that biology is destiny. Andrew had the height, but not the heart, for hoops. He loathed the physicality under the basket, where players routinely jostled for positioning and rebounds. "I didn't like going elbow to elbow with guys," Andrew said. He took the shoving personally, responding to opponents' aggression with a pained look that telegraphed what he was thinking: "Stop hurting me!"

On the fateful day that he ran for Jeff, Andrew was a senior in high school with aspirations of competing for a Division II or III program—but not in track, where he had no competitive history. He had run two years of cross-country in high school, and so a low-key program—maybe at Keene State in New Hampshire, or the University of Vermont—seemed the next logical step. Like the animals on the farms he passed on his regular running route through Norwich, his development was not rushed. No attempt was made to supersize his natural gifts. His parents, Justin and Betsy, refused to subscribe to the philosophy, gaining a wide following elsewhere, that children, if they are going to have success in athletics or music or theater, must partake of individual coaching and specialized camps and seek out the best competition from a young age. They believed that children mature at different rates, and for that reason they had to be free to indulge in many activities. "It takes all these different experiences for kids to focus on what they really want," Betsy Wheating said. Andrew changed sports with the seasons, and even though it was obvious that he enjoyed soccer the most, his parents never took his participation for granted. "My parents would ask, 'Do you want to play soccer in the spring?' and I'd say, 'Yes! Yes! Put me on the team!'" he said.

Nor did the Wheatings assume their children were destined for the sports that ran in the family bloodline. Andrew's paternal grandmother, June Goodall Wheating, was one of the best badminton players of her generation. Representing South Africa in the 1950s, she was ranked third in the world, but her sport was not included in the Olympic program at the time. Andrew's father played on the England under-22 field hockey team, a feeder program for Great Britain's national team. He was dropped from England's senior team shortly before the Great Britain squad was selected. It ultimately failed to qualify for the 1976 Summer Olympics. Ahead of the 1984 Games in Los Angeles, Justin was approached about representing the United States. As the host country, it automatically qualified for the competition.

Changing nationalities or even sports to enhance one's chances of becoming an Olympian has become a common practice, but back then Andrew's father wasn't interested. "It did not seem right to switch nationalities just to play hockey," he said. Instead, Justin poured his energies into his chosen career field.

During Andrew's childhood, his father worked as a corporate head for a company that made snowboards and later for a golf-equipment manufacturer. Before Andrew entered the eighth grade, Justin accepted a job as the chief operating and financial adviser for Simon Pearce, the renowned glassblower, which prompted the family's move from Atlanta to Norwich.

Justin's work dropped his family into the circles of some of the best snowboarders and golfers in the world, but he steered his three children into neither sport. Nor did he try to impose on them his affinity for field hockey. Andrew's parents allowed him the freedom to develop his own relationship to sports. This autonomy is fundamental to a child's growth. Developmental Psychology 101 says that kids who possess a basic sense that they are the architects of their lives will grow into happier, more resilient adults. Justin and Betsy resembled the parents of world-class musicians, artists, athletes, and scientists studied by the psychologist Benjamin Bloom, who found that parents raised superstar kids by not trying to. The group included no drill sergeants, slave drivers, or starry-eyed dreamers, just parents who responded to their children's intrinsic motivation and offered unconditional support. "Credit to my parents, really," Andrew said. "If they had pushed me into running, I probably would have burned out, like I've seen happen to other runners."

Without meaning to, Wheating's father did influence Andrew's love of soccer. When Andrew was young, his father played in an adult recreation soccer league. The sport became the glue that strengthened the father-son bond. "My dad's always been my idol," Andrew said, "so if he loved soccer, I loved soccer." If his father introduced him to the game, David Beckham, the iconic English midfielder known for his bending kicks, was the reason he fell head over heels in love with it. Andrew had Beckham's Manchester United replica jersey displayed on his bedroom wall. In his eyes, Beckham was the epitome of cool, and by playing soccer, Andrew felt hip by association.

Andrew also participated in winter sports, as most Vermonters are inclined to do, lest they go stir-crazy indoors during the two or three months when the cold is a guest that quickly wears out its welcome. And looking back, Andrew said, he could see that running courted him for years before he paid it any mind. One year, he participated in a Turkey Trot on Thanksgiving Day in another part of Vermont. He was in the third or fourth grade and finished the two-mile run in twelve minutes. "That should have been the first sign," Andrew said. But in those days, running existed only as a means to an end; it got him from point A to point B on the soccer pitch.

Andrew beat everybody down the field with his speed, but he didn't have the on-ball skills to capitalize on his quickness. In more competitive settings, Andrew would have been consigned to the sideline by talented playmakers, and not playing might have stunted his overall development. Sports gave Andrew a sense of belonging. At Kimball Union, Andrew was not a star in either basketball or soccer, but he didn't care. The camaraderie mattered more than the competition. As a high school junior, Andrew happily played on the third team in soccer, a rung below junior varsity, and the junior varsity basketball squad. He could have earned his varsity letter in hoops but chose to play against lesser competition because he could get away with taking long jumpers from the perimeter. At scores of high schools, where financial, faculty, and facility restrictions limit the number of participants to only the most skilled, there would have been no place for Andrew.

After moving to Norwich in the seventh grade, Andrew attended the public junior high in Hanover that absorbs the Marion Cross kids. But he was not a motivated student. "I just knew if he stayed in public school, he wouldn't float to the top; he'd float to the bottom," Betsy said.

Kimball Union, with its student-to-faculty ratio of six to one, impressed his parents as a better fit for Andrew than Hanover High, which his younger brother and sister attended. Kimball Union's rural fifteen-hundred-acre campus afforded Andrew the space he craved, while the close classroom supervision gave him the structure he needed.

Andrew loved how soccer provided a release valve for his pent-up energy and valued the connection he developed with his teammates. And yet the solitary sport of running kept beckoning to him. At the start of every soccer season, the Kimball Union coach required all of his players to complete a timed mile run. Andrew left his gasping teammates far behind. As a junior he clocked a time of five minutes, a pace unattainable by all but roughly 10 percent of competitive male runners.

The coach suggested that Andrew switch from soccer to cross-country. Andrew was resistant, dismissing running as nerdy, and so the coach enlisted another teacher and former competitive runner, Kevin Ramos-Glew, to help sell Andrew on the idea. "It's not like we invested in Andy because we thought he'd be an Olympian," Ramos-Glew said. "Who the hell knew?" At the coaxing of Ramos-Glew, Andrew watched *Without Limits*, a 1998 film based on the life of Steve Prefontaine, the runner who in the 1970s was

James Dean cool. Prefontaine was a stocky runner whose handsome face contorted in pain when he raced. His obvious effort was a large part of his appeal; he was a blue-chip runner with a blue-collar sensibility. Prefontaine finished fourth in the 5,000 meters at the 1972 Summer Olympics in Munich. He once held the American record in every outdoor distance race from the 2,000 meters on, in a mind-boggling display of range. Prefontaine's legend grew after he died in a car accident, at the age of twenty-four, a year before the 1976 Montreal Games.

Andrew illegally downloaded the movie onto his laptop, a move that would have earned the approval of the nonconformist Prefontaine. He was transfixed by Billy Crudup's performance. Forget Beckham—he would become the next Prefontaine. That was the end of soccer for Andrew, who competed in cross-country as a junior and won all of his local races. During his senior year, his mother did an Internet search on how to enter the 2005 Foot Locker Cross Country Championships Northeast Regional in New York, a national high school competition she had heard people mention. It sounded like kind of a big deal. Andrew entered the event and placed a respectable eighteenth. He also won his second New England small-division prep school cross-country title. His success caught the attention of Dave Faucher, the varsity basketball coach who had once headed the men's hoops program at Dartmouth College.

Forty years earlier, Faucher had first crossed paths with Jeff Johnson, who was selling sneakers out of the trunk of his car for the company that in 1971 became Nike—a name Jeff suggested, inspired by the winged goddess of victory. When Faucher saw Andrew's cross-country times, including a victory secured after a December storm dumped nearly four inches of snow on the course, he thought of Jeff. Although Faucher had Jeff's cell number, he knew better than to call it. Jeff stores his phone in the glove compartment of his Subaru and treats it like a fire extinguisher behind glass: to be used only in case of an emergency. Faucher reached Jeff on his landline and told him there was a runner at Kimball Union who appeared to have raw talent. Would Jeff take a look at him?

Jeff was intrigued. He views running as more than a sport. To him, it is a metaphysical exercise, as sacred as prayer or meditation; a vehicle for grace. Converts were always welcome. He spoke reverentially of Prefontaine, whose career he had watched unfold from the time Prefontaine was a high school runner in Coos Bay, Oregon. In 1965, Jeff was approached by Phil Knight, whom he had met when both were students at Stanford, and asked for his help with a sneaker import business he was starting. Knight, then a junior accountant, knew that Jeff, a former competitive runner, was well connected in the world of track. Jeff was working as a social worker in Los Angeles at the time, and for a while he spent his weekdays helping the downtrodden and his weekends peddling Phil's upscale sneakers at track meets.

His double life didn't last long. Two years after he joined forces with Knight, Jeff quit his day job and relocated to the East Coast, where he eventually opened the company's first shoe factory, in Exeter, New Hampshire, close to shipping ports and in the middle of an active New England running scene. In 1971, the company lost its Japanese distributor, hastening its metamorphosis from marketer to manufacturer. "It was terribly risky," Jeff said. "We had no idea how to make shoes, and there had never been quality running shoes made in America." Jeff, a natural-born entrepreneur, spent eighteen years working for Knight. The shoe company that Jeff helped launch became wildly successful, and a corporate culture replaced the quirky, entrepreneurial environment in which Jeff had thrived. In the early 1980s, at the age of forty-one, he left Nike as a kind of cult figure and retired a rich man. Years later, track aficionados showed up at meets in Europe wearing T-shirts that read, "Where's Jeff Johnson?"

He was hiding in plain sight in Lebanon, a little east of Norwich. With the financial freedom to live anywhere, Jeff settled there because it reminded him of the Northern California of his youth, an area that has since been bulldozed beyond recognition. "Every time I was away and went home, there was a new freeway or a place where I had run that was paved over," he said. "It was shocking and disturbing." The area enveloping Dartmouth College, known as the Upper Valley, appealed to Jeff, he said, "because it hasn't changed in three hundred years in a lot of significant ways. The woods are still full of animals, there's still green grass and not black pavement. In California you can't even get around anymore. It's bumper-to-bumper traffic. Why would I want that?" Jeff's decision to retire on the East Coast instead of closer to his roots made possible his serendipitous meeting with Andrew three decades later. "In Jeff, Andy just fell into the hands of the perfect person," Betsy Wheating said.

Jeff arranged to meet Andrew at the Dartmouth indoor track. Thirty-one banners hung from one wall like discolored medal ribbons on a highly decorated general's chest. Andrew couldn't stop staring at Jeff. Here was the man who named the company that produced the sneakers that Michael Jordan made famous and that Andrew wore on his feet. Andrew could not believe his good fortune. What were the odds that a man who knew almost every great track performer, including Prefontaine, would be ensconced in rural New Hampshire, a long training run from Norwich? Yet Andrew wasn't nervous in Johnson's presence. He didn't know enough about running to comprehend the stakes. Andrew stripped down to shorts, a T-shirt, and flat-soled sneakers, and Jeff wasted no time getting started. "I wanted to sort of evaluate the condition he was in," said Jeff, who suggested a set of 400s on the 200-meter track. Could Andrew manage ten repeats of two laps at a sixty-seven-to-seventy-second pace, with three minutes of rest in between? Andrew licked his lips. The dry air in the field house made swallowing difficult. He had never tackled a set of 400s. Kimball Union didn't even have a track. This was virgin territory, and he had no way of monitoring how fast he was going because Jeff had instructed him not to wear a wristwatch. Oh well, Andrew thought to himself. He'd figure it out as he went along. He took off, determined to please this taciturn stranger. "I wanted to nail it," he said.

As he watched Andrew complete the first lap, Jeff's spirits sagged. "I'm thinking, 'Oh no, he has no sense of pace at all,'" he said. Then Jeff glanced at the stopwatch hanging around his neck. It showed Andrew's 200 split, and the time was startlingly fast. He called the number out to Andrew as he ran past, his footfalls as quiet as those of the deer that routinely wandered up to the front porch of Jeff's house. Jeff shook his watch and then his head. Was this kid for real? Andrew completed the second lap, and Jeff called out the 400-meter time. "Sixty-three seconds." He forced himself to keep his voice measured. "Why don't you jog a couple of laps and come back and see if we can do that again?"

Yeah right, Jeff thought. No way could Andrew repeat that remarkable time. Convention held that you'd sooner see a billboard in Vermont than an untrained runner who can clock a single 400 in less than sixty-five seconds. But around and around the track Andrew ran, recording one sub-seventy 400 after another while Jeff tried to contain his excitement. It was like watching someone playing the piano but had no instruction in reading music. "I'm looking around like, 'Is this a dream?'" Jeff said. "I'd never seen anyone run so fast and look like he wasn't running at all. It was effortless. Totally effortless." Andrew had a long stride, and he ran with his torso school-marm straight, as if he had an apple on his head. Jeff took Andrew out for a post-workout meal and casually asked him how serious he was about running. Andrew said he intended to run in college. Puffing out his chest, he allowed that a couple of cross-country programs from schools that don't award athletic scholarships had expressed interest.

Jeff blinked at him in bewilderment. The kid didn't get it. He was settling for regional theater when he had the talent to star on Broadway. Jeff explained that he was friends with the coach at the University of Oregon, where Prefontaine had starred and where dozens of other Olympians have trained. Would it be okay if he made a call to his friend on Andrew's behalf? "Sure, go ahead," Andrew said with a shrug. Then he resumed chewing his sandwich. "I might as well have said, 'Do you mind if I call the University of Mars about you?'" Jeff said. He had to explain to Andrew that Oregon was the New England Patriots of college track—the gold standard. It shouldn't have been surprising that Andrew was clueless. For him, a college scholarship had never been a reason to run.

Starting with his parents, he had a web of support that nurtured him in a low-key manner. Years later, Andrew would look back at his organic origins as a gift. If he had started running sooner, he is not sure what, if anything, he would have gained. In college, he saw track prodigies slowed by injuries caused by the repetitive pounding on their joints. One of the United States' leading experts on youth sports injuries, Dr. Neeru Jayanthi, conducted a three-year study that found that kids whose devotion to a single sport adds up to more hours a week than their ages had a 36 percent increased risk of experiencing serious overuse injuries. Andrew also watched talented runners with more than a decade of racing behind them and seemingly bright futures quit because of burnout. He didn't appreciate it at the time, but by playing soccer and basketball deep into high school, Andrew had essentially enjoyed a generalized training program that provided a solid foundation for the specialized work he would commit to in college. He developed a strong core and improved the stability in his muscles and joints, the better to avoid injuries from repeating one set of movements. And those flying elbows under the basket that Andrew endured while playing basketball turned out to be ideal training for the jostling for position that occurs on the track. All the contact he endured in soccer prepared him for the tangle of feet he would encounter while running in a pack. His experiences in other sports had better prepared him for success on the track.

Jeff visited Andrew's parents and told them their son was a really good runner. They smiled and said, "That's nice." He told them they didn't understand: he was really, really good. Andrew's parents smiled and nodded some more. Andrew would later say how thankful he was that they were not like other parents he encountered, the ones who dissected their child's races in excruciating detail, wringing the joy from the activity with their analysis.

Andrew would later be described as potentially the best American miler since Jim Ryun in the 1960s. But in the beginning, he didn't know enough about running's history to feel any pressure. Had he been aware that no American miler had won an Olympic medal since Ryun in 1968, he might have been discouraged before he ever tried the middle distances. Andrew was such a neophyte that his "training" for cross-country races in high school often consisted of games of Ultimate Frisbee.

He spent the winter and spring of 2006 completing workouts on the track overseen by Jeff. Some of the drills Jeff devised were far off the beaten path, like when he encouraged Andrew to speed walk pigeon-toed on his heels for forty to fifty meters at a stretch to strengthen the smaller, stabilizing muscles in his feet and ankles. Andrew loved it. In Jeff, he found a mentor who viewed the track as a canvas for his imagination. They had a shared vision of the sport as both a creative and physical outlet. It didn't worry Jeff that Andrew was getting such a late start. The Norwegian Grete Waitz didn't run her first competitive race until she was well into her teens, and she went on to set world records at 3,000 meters, 8K, 10K, 15K, and 10 miles. She broke the marathon world record four times, including the first time she competed at the 26.2-mile distance.

Jeff's circle of friends also included Oregon's track coach Vin Lananna, who had served as an assistant athletic director and head coach for cross-country and track and field at Dartmouth in the 1980s. At Jeff's urging, Lananna met with Andrew at the Hanover Inn during the winter of 2006 while visiting his son, who was a student at Dartmouth. From his time in Hanover, Lananna knew the New England type, and he recognized it in Andrew: hardworking and unpretentious. But Andrew's enthusiasm for running and his kinetic energy also made an impression on Lananna, who invited him to Eugene on a recruiting visit. Upon returning home, Andrew told his mother he had changed his mind about attending Quinnipiac in Connecticut or some other small East Coast school. "I want to be an Oregon Duck," he said.

Lananna, who had still never seen Andrew race in person, offered him a two-hundred-dollar athletic scholarship. It represented a pittance of the total cost of out-of-state tuition—only enough to cover his books. But the money elevated Andrew's standing with the admissions department. He was placed in a category that fast-tracked his acceptance. "This kid better work out!" Lananna told Jeff after Andrew committed to Oregon.

Eugene reminded Andrew of Norwich, except in Oregon it was a freak weather event when they had to shovel snow from the trails to run. Drivers rolled down their car windows to yell encouragement as they passed him on the road during his training runs. Everyone was so supportive. On one of their visits to Eugene, Andrew's parents encountered him on the road on their way to meet him at a restaurant. He was headed in the same direction on his bicycle. They called out his name, but he did not react. Once they were seated at the table, Betsy asked her son why he hadn't responded. What was that all about? Andrew smiled sheepishly and explained that it had become such a regular occurrence that he had learned to ignore well-wishers' shouts to avoid interactions that might cause him to be late for training.

Andrew thrived in Eugene's nurturing environment. Jeff had identified him as a miler, and in his first two years of college, Andrew steadily improved in the middle distances, where his natural speed and his stamina from all those years of running around soccer pitches proved an ideal combination. He ran an elite-level time of 1:50 in the 800 meters as a freshman, and the next season he dropped five seconds to finish second at the 2008 NCAA Championships. The clocking came with a bonus; he qualified for the Olympic trials, which were taking place on Oregon's track less than a month later. The Olympics were so far off Andrew's radar that he could not have explained the US selection process six months before he raced for a spot on the team. He had expected to take part in the trials—as a volunteer on the crew that swooped in after races to collect hurdles from the track and return them to the equipment shed. "I was hoping to be a part of the show just kind of in a small way," he said. "Up to that point, the childlike mentality was so present." His parents were no savvier. They had no idea who the marquee names in the sport were and no conception that their son was on the cusp of becoming one. Walking onto Oregon's

Hayward Field during the Olympic trials, they passed Joan Benoit Samuelson, who had beaten Waitz to win the gold medal in the first women's Olympic marathon in Los Angeles in 1984. She saw them in their custom-designed T-shirts identifying them as members of Andrew's family and said, "Go KUA," as she passed; she knew of the small school because it was her father's alma mater. Andrew's parents thanked her for her support, and then asked a stranger next to them, "Who was that?"

On the last night in June, eight men converged on Hayward Field to compete for three berths to the 2008 Beijing Olympics in the 800-meter final. The runners stood on the track, swaying in nervous anticipation. The hometown crowd had thrown its collective voice behind Andrew in Lane 3. He had a heavy curtain of brown bangs falling in his eyes, a ghostly pallor, and hunched shoulders. With three years of racing experience, Andrew was the sapling amid the giant Douglas firs at the starting line. One of the other finalists, Jonathan Johnson, had advanced to the semifinals in the event at the Athens Olympics four years earlier and had been competing for a dozen years.

The large green *O* on Andrew's yellow singlet represented Oregon, where he was about to enter his junior year, but it could easily have reflected people's shocked expressions to see him in the mix for an Olympic berth. A record 20,939 spectators had crammed into the stadium, which was built to accommodate a few thousand less. A spillover crowd had turned the soccer stadium next door into a gigantic green-carpeted family room; a giant video screen broadcasted the live action on the track. The fans roared in surround sound as the massive video board, which faced the starting line, flashed a close-up of Andrew as he was being introduced. He waved and clapped in time with the crowd. Around his neck he wore a puka-shell necklace, a gift from one of the first friends he made after moving to Norwich. Andrew absently fingered the shells. He remembered what his friend had told him when he gave Andrew the necklace. "This is so you remember me when you're a big hotshot celebrity," he said. Andrew had laughed at the time, because he was in on the joke. In Norwich, where everybody is special, nobody is a celebrity.

The race began, and Andrew fell back into last place. The pace setter was Khadevis Robinson, a four-time US champion, 2004 Olympian, and new father. He had all the years of race and life experience that Andrew lacked. Robinson covered the first four hundred meters at a brisk clip. "Don't panic," Andrew told himself. "Stay calm." The lead runners eased up, and Andrew's mind began to race. Though still the caboose of this eight-car train, he suddenly felt in control. "I'm so going to make this team!" he remembered thinking. He was running high on his toes, and his legs felt light. With 170 meters left, the race favorite, Nick Symmonds, hanging back in seventh place, started his kick. Symmonds, born in Arkansas, raised in Idaho, and schooled at Oregon's Willamette University, trained in Eugene and had a wrestler's build. Like Andrew, he was known for his strong finish.

When Symmonds made his move, it was as if an alarm went off in Andrew's head. "It woke me up," he said. Running on the outside, he shifted into high gear and chased after Symmonds. Andrew blasted out of the last curve as if shot from a sling. The fans roared as the two runners with local connections sprinted for the finish line. With each runner that Andrew passed, the crowd noise seemed to double in decibels. By the end, it was so loud that he couldn't hear his own breath or his feet touching the track. "The noise rattled me outside my own brain," he said. The sound was like a wave that carried him across the finish line. People would later say they hadn't felt Hayward Field pulse with so much noise since Prefontaine last graced the track.

Andrew finished second behind Symmonds, who would become his training partner at the Oregon Track Club. Another Eugene-based runner, Christian Smith, dived across the finish line for a local sweep of the Olympic berths. The crowd roared like a jumbo jet. In the stands along the opposite straightaway, Andrew's parents exchanged shocked looks. On the track, Andrew's hands reflexively flew to his face. He raked his hair with his fingers, cradled his head in his arms, and looked heavenward. Then he fell to his knees. His reaction was widely interpreted as disbelief. In fact, Andrew said, he was shaken. His first thought wasn't that he had won a berth to the Olympics but that he had lost the race. "I remember not fully grasping what I had just done," he said. "I had never dreamed of making an Olympic team, so I wasn't thinking, 'I'm going to the Olympics.'" Andrew's success was so improbable that a rival coach sidled up to Lananna and joked that the scarecrow-thin Andrew must be tested at once for performance-enhancing drugs. Lananna laughed and said that Andrew wouldn't know "a steroid from a hemorrhoid."

It wasn't until a woman handed Andrew a miniature American flag that the magnitude of what he had accomplished hit him. At twenty years old, Andrew was the youngest man on the US Olympic track team. In a television interview after the race, Andrew was asked how he did it. Raising his voice to be heard above the din of the crowd, he motioned behind him and said, "It's the fans. It's all you guys." Back in Norwich, the townspeople were thrilled. Like the famed Appalachian Trail, Andrew had run through town, and now his passion had carried him all the way to the world stage in Beijing. As they had for the others, the townsfolk organized a send-off party for Andrew. More than a hundred people gathered in the pouring rain, huddled under a tent at the Upper Valley Events Center on US Route 5, across from a Subaru dealership. Andrew was the eleventh Norwich Olympian, but only the second, after the kayaker Brett Heyl in 2004, to qualify in a summer sport. It was like finding an avocado tree growing among the sugar maples.

Andrew received a variety of gifts, including the customary plastic bag of cheers, a bottle of water from Dan & Whit's, two cans of baked beans, and running spikes with a hook on them to prevent him from tumbling off the other side of the world. Andrew was touched by the quirky, highly personalized ceremony. The send-off embodied what he loved about the town, which he described as "bizarre in a good way." It was, he said, "a place where nobody wants to succeed for themselves. Everybody wants to succeed for everybody else."

As Andrew's father watched the proceedings, he reflected on how his family had come to live in such a place. They had settled in Norwich at the recommendation of his then boss, Simon Pearce, whose son Kevin was at the time one of the top snowboarders in the world. Simon told Justin Wheating that he bought a house in Norwich and commuted to his studio in Quechee, twenty minutes each way, so his boys would fall under the auspices of the Dresden School District, one of the first interstate school districts in the country and among the last acts signed into law by President Kennedy before his assassination. The district, known for its excellence, encompasses the towns of Norwich and Hanover, which educate their elementary-school-age children separately before combining them from seventh through twelfth grades. Andrew's father looked into real estate in Norwich and was dismayed to find that homes came on the market infrequently and sold quickly. He told Simon that housing prices were giving him sticker shock. Simon assured him that the single-family homes that cost upward of five hundred thousand dollars were a bargain. No price could be put on the community values and the local schools, he explained.

Justin searched for a house in Norwich with a real estate agent who warned him that properties often sold before they officially came on the market, snatched up by the sellers' friends or acquaintances. The first day, Justin put an offer on a house before his wife had a chance to tour it; his Realtor said that if he hesitated, someone else would swoop in and buy it. Betsy agreed sight unseen to the four-bedroom, three-and-a-half bath, 3,308-square-foot home after Justin assured her it was within walking distance of the elementary school. Now, years later, as they watched the town fete for Andrew, his parents had to admit that Simon Pearce had been right. Norwich was worth its square footage in gold.

Andrew's inexperience caught up to him in Beijing, where he didn't make it out of the heats after running a tactically unsound race. He had not watched the Olympics growing up, and participating in the first Summer Games he had ever seen was overwhelming. His claim to fame in China, he said with a laugh, was getting mistaken for Michael Phelps, who won a record eight gold medals in swimming. The resemblance is a stretch. With his slightly hunched posture, mop of brown hair in a perpetual state of bedhead, long body, and angular face that lights up like a lantern when he smiles, Andrew looks more like the cartoon character Norville "Shaggy" Rogers, the owner of the mystery-solving Great Dane Scooby-Doo. He has a playful personality, too. In his downtime, he and friends make funny videos that they post on social media. In the name of art, Andrew has dressed in a girlfriend's skirt and women's heels and tee-tered on a Eugene street corner at night.

The camera became Andrew's refuge from the race clock. The videos allowed him to pretend to be some-body else, which was especially therapeutic when he was struggling with the track world's expectations of his be-coming the next great American miler. Andrew has used both platforms—track and social media—to advance his stripped-down life philosophy, one that values relation-ships and adventures more than any result. "The material things that people can get from Olympic sports—living that moment on the podium with your national anthem playing, the success it brings, the money side of it, the fame—it's all temporary," Andrew said. "But the joyful-ness of doing something you love and living a rich, full life, that's something you have to look forward to every day."

In college, Andrew re-created the nurturing community he had grown up with in Norwich. The Oregon track team became his support group. After he made the 2008 Olympic team, some people encouraged him to forsake his final two years of college eligibility and turn professional. He could continue to attend classes but would have been able to accept money for races and sign lucrative endorsement deals. But Andrew wanted to help his whole college team prosper rather than enrich only himself.

Andrew competed for Oregon for all four years and capped off a decorated career with a stellar senior season. At the 2010 NCAA Outdoor Track and Field Championships, held on his home track in Eugene, Andrew became the fifth man in history to win both the 800 and 1,500, the metric equivalent of the mile, and the first since another Oregon runner, Joaquim Cruz, in 1984. Cruz went on to win the 1984 Olympic gold medal in the 800 meters. Andrew then proceeded to break Cruz's twenty-six-year-old school mile record with a personal best of 3:51.74. He had become part of an elite fraternity in US track, named in the same breath as some of the most accomplished milers. But the best was yet to come. At a meet in Monaco during his first running tour of Europe, Andrew dropped his personal best in the 1,500 meters by a startling seven seconds. His time of 3:30.90 was the second-fastest clocking by a US-born runner in history. It was within 1.6 seconds of the American record held by Bernard Lagat, who sent his congratulations on Twitter. Leonel Manzano, who had represented the United States in the event at the Beijing Olympics, finished last in the race in Monaco. But he got a second wind from watching Wheating's childlike exuberance. Andrew's reaction to setting a personal best reminded Manzano that running was supposed to be fun. He later credited that race with helping him to fall back in love with the sport. Two years later, a reenergized Manzano would win a silver medal in the 1,500 meters at the London Olympics. By the time Andrew graduated from Oregon in 2010 with a degree in sociology, he could make a comfortable living on the track. Long gone were the days of Prefontaine, who one year after his fourth-place finish at the 1972 Olympics was living with a teammate in a trailer, growing his own vegetables, and getting by with the help of government-issued food stamps. The dash for cash had become an established race, and Andrew became the subject of a bidding war between shoe companies. He met with representatives from New Balance and Nike. Andrew liked both brands. Nike was the company that his mentor,

Jeff Johnson, had helped build, but he felt an instant connection with the representatives from New Balance, headquartered in Boston, a two-hour drive from Norwich. They seemed to grasp that he ran for the joy of it, not for the fortune to be made. "The well-being of their athletes comes first, not their performance," Andrew remembered. But track's new economy created a problem for Andrew, whose club coach in Eugene was sponsored by Nike. If he chose to align himself with New Balance, he would gain a sponsor but lose his home base, because it would be awkward for a Nike coach to work with a New Balance athlete.

Andrew signed a six-figure deal with Nike that included a base salary and performance incentives. The ethos of Norwich that had helped shape him—participation over proficiency, communitarianism over competition—was out of step with the realities of his new life. To collect on performance incentives, Andrew had to vanquish fields that included the runners with whom he trained daily in Eugene. In college, his training mates weren't all milers, which alleviated the competitive tension. But from the fall of 2011 onward, Andrew worked out alongside other top milers, which gave every practice a race-day intensity. If he had a bad training session, he'd return home and brood about how well his rivals were running and what that meant for the money races. Andrew would never again feel untethered by expectations, like he had before the 800-meter final at the 2008 US Olympic trials. He watches the tape of that race on occasion and always tears up. "I sit there and wonder, 'How did I do it?'" he said. "Looking back on the racing I did when I was younger, the innocence of just purely running is so clear."

The specialization that Andrew sidestepped growing up could no longer be avoided. Running was now his job. He passed up holidays in Vermont to stay in Oregon and train. He qualified for the 2012 Olympics with a third-place finish in the 1,500 meters at the US trials—the event that Johnson had envisioned for him from the start. He made it to the semifinals at the London Summer Games, but after that, he sustained a series of injuries that stalled his progress. In 2015, Andrew recorded his first victory at a major international event when he won the 1,500 meters at the Pan American Games in Toronto. He felt more relief than joy; after all, he was being paid to perform. "The expectation is now you can't do anything great and have it be meaningful," he said, "because that's what's expected of you."

A couple of months before the Pan American Games, Andrew raced without distinction at the Prefontaine Classic, the same meet where five years earlier he had broken the school's twenty-six-year-old mile record. The next day I met Andrew for breakfast. He chose a coffeehouse in a restored Victorian in Eugene that is popular with Oregon students. It was a warm spring morning, and we sat outside on the spacious patio. Between bites of a breakfast sandwich, Andrew talked about the constant tension he feels between the purity of running and the business of track. He divided runners into two groups. The first is the ten-point group, so named because its members are inspired to win so that they can help their team succeed. Then there is the one-point group, composed of athletes whose motivation is to beat everybody for their own glorification. "I've tried, but I don't have the arrogance, the macho-man mentality, to do that," Andrew said. He is a ten-point guy, invested in winning to score as many points as he can for his team and to make his school, his coach, his family, and his community proud. "That's just how I live my life," he said. He could not relate to his training teammate Nick Symmonds, the 800 runner who beat Andrew at the 2008 Olympic trials and years later would describe running as a business and "a great way for me to market my products."

Symmonds's activism for athletes to become moving billboards, to auction their shoulders as advertising space to the highest corporate bid, stands in stark contrast to Andrew's stated desire "to do things for other people." His need for community compelled him to join the Big Brothers Big Sisters organization after the 2012 Olympics. Andrew was paired with a boy in middle school with whom he spent a couple of hours every week playing video games and performing simple tricks on a trampoline. The boy loved football and expressed a desire to improve his foot speed, so Andrew accompanied him to a field, and together they ran sprints. The boy had no idea that Andrew was an Olympic runner until stories about Andrew appeared in the local newspaper and on television and, as Andrew said, "blew my cover." He spent time with the boy on a regular basis for three years, reluctantly dropping out of the program as the 2016 US Olympic trials neared because his Big Brother obligations bled into his running schedule.

Andrew's inability to juggle his track responsibilities and the Big Brother experience gnawed at him. It served as another reminder that the athletes who fare the best

as professionals are the self-centered, one-point performers. Ever since college, Andrew said, "The challenge
for me has been how to create a collaborative motivation
when you're a professional athlete in it for yourself." He
stopped talking when he became aware that a shadow
had fallen over our table. Another breakfast customer,
a woman, was standing expectantly at his shoulder. She
apologized for bothering him. She had watched his race
at the Prefontaine meet. "I just wanted you to know that
we still love you anyway," she said. Andrew thanked her,
but the woman wasn't finished. "You looked so sad in
your interview," she said. Andrew smiled. "Not the best
race," he said. "That'll happen. That's all right." He was
three thousand miles from Norwich, but at that minute
he felt as if he could have been outside King Arthur Flour,
a bakery and café on Route 5 near the site of his 2008
Olympic send-off. The unqualified support felt warmer
on his back than the late-spring sun.

The next time I caught up with Andrew, he was driving the length of the California coast in his pickup truck.
It was the fall of 2016, three months after he had finished
twelfth in the 1,500-meter final at the 2016 US Olympic trials to miss making the team that competed in the
Rio de Janeiro Games. The winner at the US trials, Matt

Centrowitz, set a meet record of 3:34.09 and then pulled off an upset victory in Brazil. Andrew finished more than six seconds behind Centrowitz. After the selection meet, Andrew decided to change his approach. His Nike contract ran through 2017 and was structured so that he felt like a salesman working largely on commission. He had a base salary, which could be greatly enriched through performance bonuses. At the time it was drawn up, Andrew's upside was high. He was expected to compete internationally and grace medals podiums and maybe set records. Six years later, the reality is that he is not qualifying for the bonuses. "I'm not making the teams and I haven't won any medals, so naturally they're cutting me down further and further," he said. Andrew had given his life over to track, and where had it gotten him? He realized he was better off when his life had more balance.

Andrew decided to join an indoor recreational soccer league, where he ably filled the role of defensive midfielder. On occasion he'd be recognized by an opponent, who afterward would make a comment to the effect of "I'm pretty sure I've seen you do some amazing things on the track." With every game, Andrew created more distance between himself and that performer who was supposed to be the next great American miler. Out on the pitch, he felt as if he were a child again. He loved contributing to the success of his team, and after losses he enjoyed seeking out the winners and praising their efforts.

In the fall, Andrew hopped into his truck with his mutt, Boomer, riding shotgun and pointed the car south. The open road gave him license to think. "I kind of wanted to explore who I am and what I want to accomplish in life," he said. Andrew's plan was to continue to run, but not at the expense of family holidays and his happiness. "What I value most is not a gold medal," Andrew said. "The things that I value most are having a family someday and living a full life." Four months after our conversation, Andrew left the Oregon Track Club, having determined that he would be happier if he didn't have what he described as a "regimented everyday schedule." From now on, every time he raced, he would make sure he represented a simpler, more joyful, Norwich way of life.

5

FREEDOM RIDER

Lesson: *Building Resilience and Responsibility Through Risk-Taking*

The first settlers in Norwich recognized that in any organism, the early stages of development were critical. The farmers saw that calves or seedlings raised in a nourishing environment developed greater resistance to disease and were more robust. Simon Pearce is not a farmer, though his father, Philip, attempted to make a living off the land in Ireland before becoming a successful potter. During his childhood in County Cork, Simon absorbed enough lessons to fill his own golden book. He applied what he learned to raising his four children, all boys, in Vermont with his US-born wife, Pia. Simon's intuitive approach to parenting was complemented by the clinical background of Pia, who had a master's in human development and a doctorate in education. The couple's youngest son, Kevin, would credit the resilience and confidence he developed as a result of his upbringing for his recovery from a life-threatening accident.

Kevin's father was reared in Ireland in a house with no telephone or refrigerator. His family didn't own a car. His parents rejected materialism for a lifestyle that stressed creativity and utilitarian beauty. Simon's children would grow up with all the creature comforts— and then some—but also with a deep appreciation for things like family and nature that are easily taken for granted. In 1981, Pearce immigrated from Ireland to the United States and turned a renovated textile mill perched atop the falls of the Ottauquechee River in Quechee, Vermont, into a multimillion-dollar tableware empire. His glassblowing business has expanded to include a string of retail outlets and several factories. The Pearces settled on Elm Street in Norwich, a half hour's drive from the mill. They were drawn to the town by the wide-open spaces and quality public education. It was the perfect combination for their active family, which includes Andrew, Adam, and Kevin, who inherited their father's dyslexia, and David, who was born with Down syndrome. "We didn't have any sense of the athletic talent the town was known for," Pia said. "We made the move only to try to make the school experience the best it possibly could be." The Pearces bought a yellow clapboard colonial with a falling-down hay barn, which they winterized and converted into a hangout for their boys, replete with a sleeping loft, a giant recreation room with Ping-Pong and air-hockey tables, and a skateboard ramp in the back. The space provided a place for the kids to convene and configure their unstructured time for fun and camaraderie.

The barn housed a kind of utopian society created by the Pearce boys and governed by their own rules, the antithesis of the regimented, adult-supervised camps and clubs that characterize modern-day play. By design, the boys were left largely to their own devices. Simon has few fond memories of school, where his dyslexia went undiagnosed. His early classroom failures and subsequent professional success informed his philosophy that a child's best teachers are his parents, whose lessons and values provide a road map to adulthood that encourages ample detours. Simon and Pia viewed setbacks, miscalculations, and failures as stepping-stones to success.

They encouraged their children to take risks, engage in horseplay, and settle among themselves the conflicts that inevitably arose. When in doubt, they erred on the side of giving their children freedom. They were determined not to be like those parents who control their children's choices for reasons having to do with their own egos or anxieties. They intuitively sensed what a 2013 study in the *Journal of Child and Family Studies* showed: that overprotective or helicopter parents thwart a child's basic psychological need for autonomy and competence, resulting in an uptick in depression and lower life-satisfaction levels.

Paul Hastings, whose sons Jeff and Chris became Olympic ski jumpers, kept his distance. And he sometimes grew exasperated trying to follow his children's high-soaring careers in the pre-Internet era. He often had to place phone calls to the sports desks at the *Valley News* or *Boston Globe* to find out how Jeff or Chris had fared at competitions on the other side of the country or across the Atlantic. Long-distance rates were expensive, and so his sons rarely phoned home. Sometimes, it was probably just as well that Paul was kept in the dark. He told me about meeting Jeff's commercial flight home to Boston after a national competition and looking right past his son when he deplaned. Jeff had crash-landed on a jump, and his face was bruised and swollen beyond recognition. At moments like that, it was hard for Paul to keep his tone neutral and ask what happened rather than issue commands like "Stop this foolishness now!"

Like Paul, Simon and Pia refrained from telling their children what to do or steering them away from any activities. Instead, they supplied information on the consequences of various actions and allowed their children to make their own decisions. Rather than forbid them to smoke cigarettes, they explained the carcinogenic effects of long-term nicotine use. And rather than recite a list of house rules for the barn, they warned the boys that if they arrived late to school or behaved in any way that attracted the attention of the Norwich police, the barn would be shuttered. They never were forced to act on the threat. The Pearces found other like-minded parents in Norwich who shared their goal of raising children who were independent, self-motivated, and curious. "By giving kids responsibility, you show that you trust them," Simon said, "and that instills confidence."

Their youngest son, Kevin, born in 1987, was the most rambunctious. As soon as he could crawl, he scaled furniture and then jumped. "He was always in motion, and so determined and resilient," Pia said. At age five, Kevin wrote a note to a family friend, Jake Burton, the founder of Burton Snowboards. He asked for a child's snowboard, which the company didn't make. Burton produced the first one for Kevin, and it was love at first flight. Kevin participated in other sports—he played on a soccer team with the future Olympic runner Andrew Wheating—but those activities were simply how he passed the time until winter, when he could carve lines in the snow at Dartmouth Skiway. He followed his brother Adam, three years older, to Stratton Mountain School, an independent boarding school located roughly eighty miles from Norwich, which focused on college preparatory academics and competitive winter sports. Stratton Mountain is the kind of place where kids committed to making the Olympics can fine-tune their focus, but Kevin came equipped with the wide-angle lens supplied by Norwich.

The school has counted more than three dozen Olympians as students, but Kevin went there to make academics more manageable, not to hone his athletic skills. He struggled to focus in a traditional classroom setting where he was cooped up inside for most of the day. The Pearces considered themselves fortunate to have the fi-

FREEDOM RIDER

nancial means to send Kevin to a school where, as his mother said, "He got to spend the best part of the day outside on the mountain. It was truly alternative in all respects."

With his brother Adam, Kevin re-created the Norwich barn brotherhood at Stratton Mountain by seeking out friends who shared their all-for-fun, fun-for-all spirit, adhering to his family's values, which prioritized relationships over results. The snowboarding friends he made at the school would form the nucleus of his inner circle, a fellowship that would factor large in his post-accident recovery. Kevin's parents' anxiety about the ever-present dangers of snowboarding was allayed by the recognition that the sport offered their boys a release from the tyranny of their schoolbooks' tangled words. Simon and Pia recognized that their children's paths likely wouldn't take them the Ivy League route. The outside, not the classroom, was their boys' optimal learning environment. So Kevin's parents explained the consequences of various reckless behaviors, starting with not wearing a helmet, and then set their sons free. "We are firm believers in letting kids do what they love," Pia said, adding, "The boys' attitude was 'Let's have fun.' It was never about anything more than that."

Kevin later expressed gratitude to his parents for not nagging him about his mediocre grades or setting limits on his snowboarding, which he loved precisely because in the air he felt no restraints. He gave them credit for the heights he would scale in the sport. "We had this freedom," he said. "They gave us this chance to go out and do it a different way than most kids."

The leeway Simon and Pia gave their boys extended to their education. Come high school, Kevin and Adam attended Stratton Mountain, and then Okemo Mountain School in Ludlow, Vermont, in the winters, but returned to the warm embrace of Norwich, where they felt most at home, to attend the spring and fall terms at Hanover High. Kevin's close circle of friends from high school included Drake Naples, whom he met when they were on the same sixth-grade soccer team. For Drake, school came easy and sports were hard, which made him Kevin's mirror opposite. He was not a daredevil, but then, neither was Kevin. Sure, Kevin tried tricks on a snowboard that nobody else would dare try, "but it never felt reckless," Drake said. "It was always very controlled."

Studies have shown that some people have a genetic variant that predisposes them to risk-taking sports. Drake certainly wasn't one of them. Yet the risk-averse

Drake spent almost as much time with Kevin's family as he did his own during his high school years. At the Pearces' place, he felt like he had more room to grow. He would hang out in the barn with Kevin and his brothers watching Boston Celtics games on television or finishing homework. On weekends, they'd drive a John Deere tractor in the open fields, an activity his own father, whom Drake described as a natural worrier, never would have allowed. Being around the boisterous Pearce boys lowered Drake's anxiety levels. The generous portions of independence and camaraderie, offered like plates of hot food at the dinner table, nourished his growth.

Drake wouldn't fully appreciate it until later, but all the wrestling and roughhousing and insults thrown around in the barn weren't just the hyperactivity of youth; this behavior was helping the boys form deep connections. Niobe Way, an NYU professor and author of the 2011 book *Deep Secrets: Boys' Friendships and the Crisis of Connection*, considers the teenage years all too often a transition into isolation. As boys prepare to strike out on their own, they are steered away from relationships and toward achievement. And yet emotional connections can ease the path to success. In 2008, researchers at the University of Virginia gathered thirty-four students at the base of a steep hill and fitted them each with a weighted backpack. Asked to estimate the steepness of the hill, those standing next to friends gave lower estimates than those who were alone. The longer the friends had known each other, the less steep they perceived the hill.

Kevin was rarely by himself on a mountain. He traveled in a small pack with friends and fellow competitors, including a few he knew from Stratton Mountain, as well as his brother Adam. They called themselves the "frends," leaving out the *i* because their brotherhood transcended their individual identities. They traveled without a coach, so they helped one another learn new tricks. Snowboarding's popularity as a mainstream sport had made it more competitive, less collegial. The "frends" made it their mission to focus on the fun and camaraderie that formed the sport's roots.

At eighteen, Kevin became a pro snowboarder. He signed endorsement contracts with companies including Burton, Nike, and Oakley. In 2008, two years after he graduated from Hanover High and two years before the next Winter Games, he won three medals at the X Games, an Olympic-style event conceived and aired by ESPN. In the next two years, Kevin established himself as the principal challenger to Shaun White, the

2006 Olympic champion snowboarder and dominant half-pipe performer. But having fun remained Kevin's main motivation. "My goal is to make people be like, 'Wow, I want to go out and try that,'" he said in the lead-up to the 2010 Vancouver Games. But as those Olympics approached, Kevin's objectives also included unseating White as the Olympic champion, which required attempting ever more difficult tricks. Kevin knew the risks. He was experiencing more crashes in practice, and told his family he planned to scale back after the Olympics. But all athletes know how thorny it can be to strike a balance between staying safe and seeking the adrenaline rush that comes from pushing boundaries.

Kevin competed on half-pipe runs that look like frozen curled cookie sheets, with the sides rising as high as twenty-two feet. Riders gain speed as they glide from one side to the other and launch themselves over the edges for jumps that can include 1,080-degree rotations. The three-man US Olympic half-pipe team was selected based on the results of five qualifying events, starting in late 2009. Kevin had been slowed by an ankle injury earlier in the year, and at the first qualifying event, at Copper Mountain, Colorado, he crashed and sustained a concussion, at least the fourth of his career. His brain was not right—he was experiencing dizziness, blurred vision, and headaches—but he told no one because he didn't want to imperil his Olympic prospects by missing any more training or sitting out any competitions. His sponsors had invested considerable sums in him. He didn't want to let them down. "All the pressure was on me because I was this guy who was going to make it to the Olympics, and I was going to win," Kevin said. "So I got up there, I kept riding."

On December 31, 2009, Kevin and his friends were in Park City, Utah, for training. Looking back, he can see that the concussion he had sustained less than two weeks earlier—and the responsibility he felt to his sponsors—set the stage for what happened next. He was performing one of the more difficult tricks, a variation of a twisting double backflip, when he slammed his forehead on the edge of the half-pipe structure and was knocked unconscious. He was wearing his helmet, which almost certainly saved his life.

Kevin was airlifted to a hospital. His brain had suffered a massive trauma. His parents, who had already arranged their travel to Vancouver for the Olympics, rushed instead to Utah to be at his side. When they arrived, they saw Kevin connected to two dozen wires and tubes, clinging to life. He spent ten days in a coma, during which tens of thousands of fans kept vigil on a Facebook page created by his brother Adam. After waking, Kevin spent more time in critical care. Forty-eight days after his accident, he watched the Olympic half-pipe competition on television from a brain rehabilitation center in Colorado with Adam, whose own competitive career had been cut short four years earlier because of a ruptured spleen and hairline fractures in his back. Adam had been working as a snowboarding instructor in Utah at the time of Kevin's accident. He quit his job, and for the next two years, as Kevin relearned how to walk, talk, and swallow, he seldom left his brother's side. "It amazed me how well he let the Olympics go," Adam told me. "It was like, 'I've got new goals to conquer.'"

At the Vancouver Games, Kevin's fellow Norwichian Hannah Kearney won the gold in the women's moguls. During the homecoming parade held for Hannah, the people of Norwich also honored Kevin, who was still in Colorado. They held up signs of encouragement, including a banner that read "You're an Olympic Hero in Our Hearts." After Kevin returned home to continue his recovery, the town threw him a party, a substitute for the Olympic send-off that had been in the works. The townspeople didn't treat Kevin any differently after the accident, which hastened his return to normalcy.

"The support was unbelievable," Pia said, and Kevin's doctors credited all the encouragement he received for his remarkable progress. Kevin returned to his snowboard 712 days after the accident. His initial refusal to accept that his competitive career was over accounted for a few of the more wrenching moments in *The Crash Reel*, a documentary chronicling Kevin's accident and recovery. During a family intervention around the kitchen table in Vermont, he tried to explain snowboarding's hold on him. "I love it, just the feeling it gives me," he said. "To be honest, I just feel like no one else in this room has that feeling about anything. Maybe Dad does about blowing glass, but it's so different than blowing glass." He tried to continue but was interrupted by Simon, who told Kevin it sounded as if he was describing an addiction. Simon posed this hypothetical: What if Simon had a pack-a-day cigarette habit and, after being urged to quit by his family, declared he would continue to smoke one or two cigarettes a day because he liked the sensation. Would Kevin be fine with that?

Simon also said he blamed himself for Kevin's accident. It was one thing to champion his son's growth and independence through risk-taking activities, but he felt as if he should have stepped in when Kevin amped up the difficulty of his tricks in response to outside expectations to raise the bar in the sport and challenge White for the Olympic gold medal. "I'll never forget when we got to the hospital," Simon said in *The Crash Reel*. "It was the one time when I broke down and felt a deep sense of responsibility for what had happened, because the pressure to perform at that level, it's very hard to get out of it."

For her part, Pia wishes she had educated herself earlier about concussions. She was so unversed in head injuries, she said, that one time when Kevin crashed on his board and was experiencing headaches and dizziness, she didn't remember taking him to the hospital. When her boys were young, if she had known what she has come to learn about blows to the brain, she would not have steered them away from snowboarding. She is clear on that. But she would have insisted that before every winter season they undergo baseline testing, a computerized assessment that measures reaction time, memory capacity, speed of mental processing, and executive functioning of the brain. That way, if they had any crashes, they could be tested and their scores compared to their baseline numbers as part of a concussion-management protocol. "I would do that piece dramatically different," Pia said.

Kevin hates that his parents feel any responsibility for his crash. The Love Your Brain yoga, meditation, and awareness program that Kevin and Adam have taken on the road to thirteen states and Canada begins with a shortened version of *The Crash Reel*, including the scene where Simon claims culpability for Kevin's accident. Several times a year, Kevin shares his story with survivors of traumatic brain injuries and their loved ones, which means that several times a year he watches *The Crash Reel* clip and relives his father's guilt. It never gets easier to sit through. "That movie's hard for me to watch, and that part is really hard because the accident wasn't my parents' fault," he told me. "I was the one out there pushing. I wanted to do it."

It was the spring of 2017, and I had caught up with Kevin in Phoenix, where more than a hundred people had convened at the Arizona Science Center for an event billed as a conversation with Kevin. The guest speaker resembled neither version of the Kevin in the documentary—the cocksure pre-injury performer and the person with the broken brain struggling with his new reality. He mingled easily with audience members, a few of whom were fellow traumatic brain injury survivors. He offered suggestions for breaking into public speaking to a twenty-three-year-old Arizona woman whose right side is paralyzed from a stroke she suffered as a high school senior. He told a young man who had been shot in the head that the best piece of advice he had to offer was "to listen to those around you, because they know a lot more than you." To another young man who got his attention and then forgot his question, Kevin counseled him not to get frustrated because that would invite negative self-talk, and negative self-talk, he said, "is not going to help you get better."

At the Phoenix event, Kevin asked for a show of hands of how many audience members had broken a bone in their bodies. A few dozen hands shot into the air. Then he asked how many are reminded of that broken bone every single day. Everyone's hands remained in their laps. When you break your brain, Kevin said, pointing to his head, it is different. "You're reminded every single day," he said, "and that's damn hard."

I thought back to the first time I met Kevin. It was in the fall of 2015, at his father's Quechee store. We made plans to meet for lunch the next week, which he canceled, with apologies, after he dropped his smartphone and it shattered, necessitating an emergency trip to the store for a replacement. This was his new normal. Whereas Kevin once routinely blew people's minds with his dexterous acts high above the ground, he was now maddeningly clumsy. He routinely broke tablets and smartphones by knocking them off tables while reaching for them, a consequence of his double vision.

The next time I saw Kevin was a year later at a San Diego, California, fund-raiser for the foundation. He was wearing dark-blue casual pants and a long-sleeve white shirt with horizontal blue stripes, Nike sneakers, and black-rimmed prescription Oakley glasses. He stood leaning in to his girlfriend of two years, Rose Farley, who was raised in Massachusetts but whose grandmother is a longtime resident of Norwich. After Kevin left her side to greet a group of volunteers, she scrolled through the photographs on her phone until she found the shot she was looking for: a helmeted Kevin riding his snowboard at Mt. Mansfield in Stowe, taken three days earlier. His expression radiated childlike joy. Rose doesn't worry about Kevin's safety. "He's really smart about it," she said.

Life is neither easy nor safe, a point driven home by those who argue that our obsession with protecting our children from harm is producing adults ill-equipped to prosper in a world that rewards the tough and tenacious. In the aftermath of Kevin's crash, critics deemed participants in demonstrably dangerous sports—and those who market, watch, and cover them—irresponsible. But it is not just the so-called adventure sports that pose risks. Kevin has listened to the stories of people who suffered traumatic brain injuries when they were hit by a car while riding a bicycle or from repeatedly heading balls in soccer. Pia said she heard from someone who sustained a traumatic brain injury while seated on an airplane when a passenger retrieving a piece of luggage from an overhead compartment dropped it on his head.

As Kevin mingled with the cocktail crowd in San Diego, my mind wandered to his father's Quechee showroom, where a back table is filled with blown-glass candle globes that I had picked up and admired. The beautiful pieces were seconds, with flaws imperceptible to the untrained eye. Kevin suffers from lingering effects of the accident, but they escaped the notice of the roughly 150 guests gathered for the event. To look at Kevin was to see the same thick mop of hair we remembered from his television close-ups; the same likable, laid-back lad whose charisma could not be contained by the small screen. His family and friends notice the changes—the tremor when he is overtired, the clumsiness caused by his lingering double vision, his sieve of a short-term memory. But they see the positive changes, too. Kevin is more outgoing and gregarious, ready to strike up a conversation with anyone. Before, he was reserved, to the point where people sometimes perceived him as aloof. His mother would never wish what happened to Kevin on anyone, but there was an upside that no one could possibly have foreseen: he emerged from the accident a better person. "Before, I wasn't doing anything important," he told me. "I was helping me. I was going out and winning all these events and all this money, but I wasn't helping that many people."

In giving back to other brain injury survivors, Kevin has grown, and strengthened, the Norwich daisy chain of support. The community impacted by traumatic brain injuries was desperate for a spokesman, and Kevin has stepped in enthusiastically to fill the void. As he told me the first time we met, "There's a lot more to life than landing a trick." He talked to the audience in San Diego for ten minutes, opening his address by announcing that

2,543 days had passed since his accident. He said he decided early in his recovery "to take whatever it was that got me to the top of snowboarding and use it to get me to the top of healing," and credited the constancy of his family's love and support for helping him endure. Kevin is convinced that his upbringing left him uniquely prepared for his post-accident life. From his brother David, whose Down syndrome presents constant challenges, he learned patience and perseverance. From his parents' desire to foster their children's independence, Kevin long ago developed the resilience and confidence that have helped him carve out a second act more meaningful than his first.

What makes Kevin stand out now is not the invincibility that his aerial tricks once hinted at but the vulnerability that he radiates. Imagine, Adam said, having a film made that captures the worst moment of your life, and then watching that film over and over for four years, reliving the horror to give others with brain injuries hope. Kevin's willingness to show his sensitive side has worn off on his brother. Kevin told the San Diego crowd that Adam's tear ducts are so flood-prone, he has been dubbed "Sad-am."

The audiences in both San Diego and Phoenix seemed

genuinely inspired by Kevin's message. I spoke to a woman who had enrolled in the yoga seminar affiliated with the event so that she could help her mother, who has a traumatic brain injury. I met a woman whose brother has a brain injury, and a young man recovering from a brain injury who traveled to San Diego from Spokane, Washington, to listen to Kevin speak. He supplied them with information, support, and, above all else, hope. Pia had told me earlier about the hundreds of letters Kevin receives from people like the recovering anorexic who told him that his story motivated her to begin eating meals again.

Toward the end of the San Diego event, Mike Sherbakov, a Marine Corps veteran who teaches yoga, led the audience in a ten-minute meditation. At one point, the reverie was broken by a pinging alarm from a smartphone. After Kevin returned to the stage, he made a confession. It was his alarm, which is set to go off every two hours to remind him to change his prescription eyeglasses. He is alternating between glasses at the suggestion of the latest doctor endeavoring to correct Kevin's double vision. He has refused to accept the conclusion of other eye specialists that his double vision is permanent. "We know so much," he said, "but we know so little."

Kevin continued to answer questions from the audience when he was interrupted by Siri, the artificial intelligence assistant, whose voice escaped from an audience member's tablet a few rows in front of me: "Sorry," Siri said, "I didn't get that." A titter rippled through the crowd, and Kevin didn't miss a beat. "Sorry, I didn't get that, either," he said, his voice rising like a revival preacher's. "I didn't get that handstand I tried to do in yoga this morning. I don't get why I see two of you whenever I look down. I don't get it. But I get that I'm okay with it; that I'm in a perfect place right now; that I'm so happy to share this experience with you."

6

THE FUTURE OF NORWICH

Lesson: *Times Change, but Time-Tested
Values Don't Have To*

The next athlete to receive an Olympic send-off on the Norwich town green could be a transplant, Julia Krass, who has taken to the rich soil like a McIntosh. But like the variety of apple that made its way down from Canada and has prospered in Vermont's Tunbridge soil, today's Norwich athletes are up against stiff competition cultivated to produce more and ripen earlier. Julia has already been to one Olympics, making her debut in Sochi in 2014 at the age of sixteen as a resident of the neighboring town of Hanover. Julia's parents moved to New Hampshire not long after an experience on a suburban

soccer field gave them a sobering glimpse of their children's futures in youth sports.

When the elder of Julia's two brothers, Pierson,
was in kindergarten, he played on a recreational league
team in Wilton, Connecticut. During one of his games,
a teammate crumpled to the ground after a collision. To
the Krasses' horror, the boy's mother screamed at him to
get up. Julia's mother was so unnerved by the incident
that she stopped attending the games. After awhile, the
Krasses began plotting their departure lest they become
infected by the same rabid parenting strain. "The madness had to stop," Julia's father, Peter, said. They left
Connecticut when Julia was a toddler. During their first
winter in New Hampshire, Julia's mother, Diana, taught
her to ski at Whaleback Mountain in nearby Enfield.

I met Julia on the soccer pitch in the fall of 2014. She
was a senior captain of the Hanover High girls' soccer
team, which was practicing on its home field ahead of
its first playoff game. It was Halloween, and the cos-
tumed ghouls and goblins were already descending on
the neighborhood as I settled into the bleachers with
an open notebook in my lap. My attempts to reach the
coach, Doug Kennedy, had been unsuccessful, so my
plan was to wait until after practice, introduce myself,

and see if it might be possible to talk to Julia. At a shade under six feet with long blond hair gathered in a pony-tail, Julia was easy to identify among the gaggle of girls. As I watched Kennedy put the players through their paces, I noticed Julia glowering in my direction. There was no mistaking that I was the object of her scorn: I was the only one in the stands. A half hour into the practice, Kennedy jogged over to the bleachers and gruffly asked if he could help me. His stern expression softened when I introduced myself and explained my earlier attempts to connect with him. He said I was welcome to stay. After practice, Julia approached me, wearing sweatpants, a hoodie, and an apologetic smile. "I'm sorry I glared at you earlier," she said. "We thought you were a spy."

For Julia, the state Division II playoffs were a big deal. Soccer was her lifeline to a normal adolescence. The year before, Julia had chosen home study over classroom learning. She would be competing on the months-long US national freestyle skiing circuit, and since she would be away from home for long stretches, the online classes made sense. By state law, she remained eligible for extra-curricular activities at Hanover High, and soccer allowed her to bond with her nonskiing school friends. Her parents had harbored reservations about Julia abandoning the classroom. They were concerned it would be difficult for her to return to a traditional learning setting in college. But they offered their input only when asked.

They brought up their children to make their own decisions. Julia's specialty, slopestyle skiing, made its Olympic debut in 2014, but Julia didn't think she had a real shot at qualifying for those Games. While her skiing rivals were applying for passports and visas, Julia's focus was on Hanover High's 2013 soccer season, which ended one victory short of the final. Her passport expired and she forgot to renew it, which wasn't that surprising; when it came to skiing, her focus was firmly on having fun.

She has always associated skiing with pleasure. From the time Julia learned the basics from her mother, the sport was a family activity for the Krasses. Alex, the brother closest to Julia in age, gravitated toward freestyle skiing. Whichever aerial move he did, Julia tried to copy. A neighbor Julia's age also liked freestyle skiing, and so, as was the case with the Hastings and Holland brothers, the sport became the most communal of individual pursuits. At Whaleback, where her family skied, Julia had the good fortune to fall under the tutelage of Evan Dybvig, a two-time US Olympian who was part of a group that bought the Whaleback ski resort in 2005.

She was eight years old and being coached by someone who had competed at the highest level of the sport. The opportunity to receive instruction from an Olympian enchanted Julia. It was like learning magic tricks from a wizard. At the recommendation of Hannah Kearney, Julia later joined the freestyle program at the Waterville Valley resort in New Hampshire, which was operated by Bill Enos, who would serve as a US Olympic coach in Sochi. Julia's specialty, slopestyle skiing, is included in the freestyle category and in some ways is the winter sport version of the steeplechase, with courses featuring obstacles such as rails, jumps, and bumps.

Most of Julia's competitions were in the West, prompting her to make another move that, like her decision to continue her schooling online, was rooted in practicality. Rather than travel back and forth from Hanover, she lived with a host family in Park City, Utah, where she had access to the state-of-the-art venues built for the 2002 Winter Olympics. The Salt Lake City Games, and the facilities it left behind, have contributed to the westward shift in US skiing, as have the more luxuriant snowfalls in the higher-elevation resorts in Utah and Colorado. A lack of snow due to rising temperatures has become a problem in New Hampshire and Vermont. In the winter of 2015, warmer weather forced the cancellation of a kids' clinic that Julia was scheduled to conduct at Whaleback. She ruefully noted those conditions, the only demonstration she would have been able to lead the kids in was calisthenics.

There was another reason that Julia's move to Park City made sense. Slopestyle skiing has less in common with Alpine skiing than with extreme sports like motocross and skateboarding, with their emphasis on pushing the limits of performance. As top performers introduce harder tricks, everybody must practice more to keep pace with the degree of difficulty. In Utah, Julia had easy access to the best slopestyle courses—much like the ski jumpers in Norwich did in the 1970s before the dismantling of the Dartmouth jump. So, usually starting around Thanksgiving, she could practice every day during the season. Hannah told me that when she made her first freestyle skiing Olympic team in 2006, she was essentially a part-time athlete. In the past decade, she said, the competition has gotten so much tougher that she doubted it would be possible for anyone to dominate the sport with the training regimen that had worked for her then.

Julia's event was added to the Olympic program as

part of a concerted effort by organizers and their television broadcasting partners to appeal to a younger, hipper demographic. Slopestyle skiing wasn't exactly lacking exposure before. It was already part of the X Games, but the Olympics would introduce the sport to a massive, mainstream audience. Julia knew the exposure would be huge, but she didn't seriously expect to take a bow on the Sochi stage. She was considered a long shot for one of the US berths. And so, with no expectations to drag her down, Julia soared. In a pep talk before the last qualifying competition, she told herself, "All I can do is what I know how to do, so I might as well go for it." Julia won the event after landing a difficult trick with two and a half revolutions that she had never performed outside of practice.

With the victory in Park City, Julia secured the fourth and final Olympic spot—and then scrambled to renew her passport and obtain a visa in time to travel to Sochi with her teammates. Of all the artful maneuvers Julia performed to get to Russia, none was more difficult than securing the appropriate documentation. She flew home with her parents for one day, which was how long it took to enlist her local congresswoman to help fast-track her visa application.

The detour allowed her time to be feted in a hastily arranged send-off ceremony that echoed the message Norwich has regularly delivered. Julia's Whaleback coach, Dybvig, said the community was proud of her and added, "There are no expectations or pressure. We just want you to do the best you can at this time of your life and enjoy representing your country on this world stage." A student-made banner was hung in the Hanover High cafeteria with handwritten messages for Julia, who advanced to the finals in Sochi and finished eleventh. She was the youngest member of the US team. When Julia and other members of the US Olympic contingent visited the White House, President Obama remarked on her youthfulness.

The White House visit made for a jarring reentry to teenage life, like returning to high school after a trip to the moon. While her classmates were studying twentieth-century American history, Julia was accepting compliments on her performance from the forty-fourth president. Her focus until then had been on enjoying her life, not building a résumé. At that moment in the East Room, Julia felt as if she had scaled the Denali of sports. She was glad she had her own personal Everest—college—to tackle next. Otherwise, it would have been easy to feel as if her post-Sochi journey was going to be all downhill.

The professionalization of Olympic sports—and the greater commitment of time, energy, and resources required to keep up—has created an environment in which anyone not actively working to become better at a sport is getting worse. The relentless march of progress was highlighted eleven months after Julia's Olympic debut when a fourteen-year-old snowboarder became the youngest X Games gold medalist. Because the competition never rests, Julia's ski coaches were adamantly opposed to her participating in high school soccer during her senior year. They didn't care that it was skiing's off-season. They wanted Julia to attend conditioning camps with other members of the US slopestyle team in Australia or New Zealand, where they could take advantage of winter conditions.

In defiance of her coaches—and in a nod to the Norwich way—Julia rejoined the Hanover High soccer team as a midfielder, a position she favored because it allowed her to distribute the ball to her teammates. It was important to her, she said, to be a normal teenager whenever possible. Besides, with the previous soccer season ending with a loss in the semifinals, Julia felt as if she had unfinished business. So she trained two hours a day with her soccer teammates and then worked out on her own to stay in shape for skiing. After Hanover won the Division II state title, the happiest player in the victory pile was Julia. She felt certain her self-imposed break, far from thwarting her progress, would enable her to return to skiing feeling recharged. But the double life she leads is occasionally exposed. Her high school team's quarterfinal game came down to penalty kicks, and as Julia lined up for her attempt—which she converted—the crowd broke into a chant of "U-S-A."

Looking back at their daughter's eventful 2014, Peter and Diana Krass were proudest that she gained admittance to Dartmouth as a member of the class of 2019. Her decision to finish high school with online classes hadn't hurt her academic standing. The Krasses viewed college as the connective span that would convey their daughter from the sports mountaintop to the vale of mortals. It was a bridge that Julia had never given much thought to having to cross until February 2015, when she caught too much air on a jump during a training run on Northern California's Mammoth Mountain, landed hard, and tore the ACL and meniscus in her right knee.

The rehabilitation was arduous. Her right leg muscles atrophied during the time she spent on crutches. It was a while before she could contemplate skiing again. And yet Julia spoke of her torn ACL with the same nonchalance as a copy-machine vendor might describe a paper cut. "Almost everyone tears their ACL at one time or another," she said.

To her, the injury was just one of the pockets of turbulence that are unavoidable when cruising at high altitudes.

Julia was still rehabilitating her knee when she started classes at Dartmouth in the fall of 2015. She relished the college experience for the opportunity it afforded to broaden her intellectual horizons and make friends outside of skiing. She took winter quarters off to train out West and compete on the international circuit, but she was adamant about not letting skiing take over her life. Her parents applauded her approach. As Julia's father told me, "If she wants to drop sports and concentrate on schooling, we'd be fine with that."

With her lithe build and wholesome looks, Julia could pass for a fashion model, which made her attractive to sponsors like Monster Energy. But Julia is not fixated on money. She realizes few Olympic athletes will accrue enough wealth to live comfortably ever after. She identifies not as a capitalist competing for riches but as an artist, with the snow as her canvas and herself as the brush. She will sometimes conjure tricks when she's in the air, relying on her feel and creative instincts rather than following a script. "My sport is very spontaneous," she said. "You do what you want, and I really like that." In her unwillingness to be hemmed in—by convention, expectations, or gravity—Julia resembles previous generations of Norwich's children. She officially became part of the town after the Sochi Games when her parents, looking to downsize and to stay close to hiking trails, moved to Norwich.

Less than two miles separate the town centers of Norwich and Hanover, but as soon as the Krasses crossed the Connecticut River, they felt as if they had entered a different world. In Norwich, Julia's father said, there is much more of a live-and-let-live attitude. People aren't judgmental. He can finish a hike and stop in at Dan & Whit's without first going home to clean up, and no one cares. This laid-back attitude extends to the care and governance of children. Whenever Julia's parents drive by the elementary school at recess, they are struck by the students frolicking on the playground no matter how foul the weather. In Hanover, Peter Krass said, if it is too cold or icy, the children are kept indoors to play to guard against accidents or injuries. In Norwich, he said, "It's a little more rough-and-tumble." Space is valued in Norwich, and not just rolling hills, nature trails, and the outdoors. The townspeople appreciate having room to explore, to breathe, to live as they choose, and they grant their children the same courtesy.

Still, the landscape is changing. Heyl, the kayaker, told me in a conversation from Denver where he is living that his ultimate dream is to return to Norwich someday and buy his childhood home, where his memories include trying to replicate the Fenway Park groundskeeper's handiwork while mowing the expansive backyard and communing with deer, groundhogs, wild turkeys, and, on one occasion, a marauding moose. But the home prices might be out of range. In 2017, a proposed project that would develop 350 acres on Route 5 across from King Arthur Flour into affordable housing and retail space was the subject of intense debate. Chris Hastings, the Olympic ski jumper, said that when he was looking to settle down, he considered living out West, in Colorado or Utah. But the ease of living there, and the insipid good cheer that it inspired, grated on him. He quickly tired of people saying, in parting, "Have a nice day." Not every day is nice, he said. Chris established his chiropractic office in Norwich, but he did not move there. He lives with his wife and children in the neighboring town of Thetford, which he described as more rural and more relaxed—more like the Norwich of his youth. Between five and seven houses, on average, are built in Norwich every year; over time this has been enough to subtly change its character. "It's more gentrified now," Chris said. "There are more type-A personalities and less open space." While I was living in Norwich, I stumbled upon a story that bolstered Chris's contention that Norwich's simple ways and generosity of spirit may be waning: a thief had stolen a row of organic broccoli, seventy pounds in all, from the fields of a Norwich farmer.

Beth Reynolds, the children's librarian at the Norwich Public Library, said the town hasn't changed at its core. It's still a community-oriented place where no one is outwardly striving to keep up with the Kardashians (or, in Norwich's case, TV's Captain Kangaroo, who until his death owned one of the more ostentatious homes, a Southern-style Tudor on several acres on Willey Hill Road). What is different, Reynolds said, is the town has become more transient. Families will settle in the area because a parent has accepted a job at Dartmouth College or the Dartmouth-Hitchcock Medical Center, and after a few years they'll move on as the parent climbs the career ladder. As home prices and property taxes continue to increase, longtime residents on a fixed income are leaving to make way for new arrivals. "You'd get to know people because families would stay for generations," Hannah said. "That's not the case anymore."

With all the new faces, it becomes harder to maintain old habits. When Jeff Hastings and Mike Holland competed in a World Cup jumping event in Lake Placid in December 1983, the townspeople pooled their resources and chartered a bus to New York to watch "their boys" compete. Thirty-two years later, Hannah also competed alongside the world's best in a freestyle skiing event in Lake Placid. A few neighbors carpooled to the event to cheer her on to a third-place finish.

Longtime residents may bemoan the big-city ex-pats in their fancy cars—and in Norwich, anything other than a utilitarian Subaru qualifies as showy—who speed along Turnpike Road and complain about the smell from the manure farmers spread in their fields. But the Huntley Meadow sports fields are where the old-timers and the newcomers find common ground, united in their resistance to the professionalization of youth sports that is becoming the norm elsewhere. After all, the desire to give their children a less stressful, more joyful existence is precisely what attracted many of the newcomers.

Can its organic model continue to thrive in 2018 and beyond? The next generation of competitive athletes, led by Brook Leigh, is eager to find out. Brook participated in the Olympic send-off for Hannah Kearney in 2010 as a fourth grader at Marion Cross. Like the other Norwich athletes, Brook refuses to focus solely on skiing. He plays on the soccer and lacrosse teams at Hanover High, not wanting to miss out on making friends outside of skiing—"people you otherwise wouldn't get to know," he said. As Brook saw it, he would have been working out anyway to maintain his overall fitness. Soccer in the fall and lacrosse in the spring allowed him to stay in shape "in a much more fun way," he said.

I first heard about Brook from a few women at a Tracy Hall exercise class, who suggested I contact Eydie Pines, one of the class's regular attendees. Her son, Brook, they said, was an up-and-coming moguls skier. The first time I talked to him was shortly before his sixteenth birthday. It was the day after a Hanover High freshman team soccer match in which he had played as a reserve. We sat in the den of his family's house in Norwich. His mother was home but stayed out of the way, joining the conversation only when summoned by Brook to supply a name or date that he couldn't remember.

Like Julia, Brook skied at Whaleback, where he was captivated by Evan Dybvig, whom he described as a dynamic coach. He also now divides his year between Vermont and Utah. Where Brook's path diverged from Julia's is that he continues to attend regular school. A straight-A student, Brook makes hopscotching between schools in Hanover and Park City look elementary, when, in fact, it takes much effort to pull off. The transfer from one high school to another and back requires an avalanche of paperwork. Brook's parents put him in charge of the details. He has to coordinate classes with his teachers at both schools, a responsibility that has fostered his sense of independence.

Whenever he returns to Park City, he faces a period of adjustment in the classroom and on the slopes—especially on the slopes, where he joins year-round freestyle skiers whose young lives revolve around the sport. They do more advanced tricks, and sometimes he feels as if it takes all winter to catch up. He doesn't worry that he's falling behind, though, because he has seen enough kids burn out as teenagers to appreciate the value of maintaining a more balanced life. He cannot imagine becoming a full-time resident of Park City, with a population more than twice Norwich's. The larger populace makes Brook feel penned in. "I like being in the wilderness," he said.

Brook was the youngest male entrant at the 2015 United States Freestyle Championships in Steamboat Springs, Colorado. It was his first national competition—and the last for Hannah, who retired shortly thereafter. The following year, during a training run in Park City, Brook hit a mogul with his left leg hyperextended. The force of the landing shredded ligaments in his left knee, requiring surgery. His rehabilitation lasted several months, leaving Brook with ample time to revisit his commitment to freestyle skiing. Were the gains worth the pain? Absolutely, he said. "I love what I'm doing," he said, "and I get more out of pushing forward than I would from playing it safe." His risk-taking resulted in a tangible reward the following winter when Brook, now seventeen, placed second in the dual moguls at the 2017 US Junior Freestyle Championships.

Brook's sentiments reminded me of something that

ski jumper Mike Holland said about working with young-sters. He told me it was rewarding to share with them what he had learned about "an unnatural sport that teaches a lot of life lessons, like confronting fear." That is the way they talk in Norwich, where the road is unknown but the way is clear.

EPILOGUE

As I walked through the glass doors of the George F. Haines International Swim Center, I smelled chlorine and eau de mildew, the bouquet of my childhood. Forty years fell away like a loosely knotted towel. It was an hour before first light, and teenagers from the Santa Clara Swim Club were turning over laps like numbers on an odometer in the largest of three pools on land where prune-plum orchards once bloomed. Before I had ever set foot in Vermont, I could identify the distinguishing characteristics of the Norwich Olympic tree, because in its roots I recognized my own.

Colonized by the Spanish, who founded Mission

Santa Clara de Asis in 1777, the city in its first hundred years was populated by farmers whose labor transformed Santa Clara into America's produce aisle. Shortly after the transcontinental railroad was completed, a Santa Clara grower named Levi A. Gould shipped California's first carload of fresh fruit east in 1869. From Santa Clara's fertile soil sprouted an industry that sent canned and dried apricots, pears, peaches, cherries, and plums all over the United States and abroad.

By the 1960s, the fruit orchards were being plowed under to make way for homes stacked like stucco dominoes. Soon after we moved to Santa Clara in the early 1970s, the apricot orchards that perfumed our neighborhood disappeared. In their place rose more houses built for people like my father, a salesman who called on companies like Intel and Hewlett-Packard. He was part of the second wave of tech migrants, drawn to the area by the semiconductor chip and the new worlds it created. The resultant electronics industry created an entrepreneurial Eden known as Silicon Valley. But those drawn to Santa Clara to cultivate lines of coding instead of rows of fruit trees brought with them a more self-serving ethos, embodied by impatient Ayn Rand–reading disruptors whose mantra is "Get it started, get it sold, and move on." The city's wide-open spaces and communitarian bedrock have given way to an overcrowded commuter culture. Santa Clara's population has exploded, the total number of residences nearly doubled. So many landmarks from my youth are gone. But the Santa Clara of my childhood still exists in a fifty-meter pool where a few dozen teenagers were practicing before school in a routine unchanged in the last fifty years.

The Santa Clara Swim Club, founded by George Haines in 1951 with thirteen swimmers, has produced eighty Olympians. During his three decades at the helm, Haines would coach more than two dozen Olympians, including Mark Spitz, the most decorated swimmer in Olympic history until Michael Phelps left him in his wake. In 1968, Spitz was one of fifteen club members to grace the US team that competed in the Mexico City Olympics. The Santa Clara swimmers won thirty-four medals at those Games, which would have placed the club third in the overall country medals count.

I once harbored aspirations of becoming another of Haines's Olympians. Inspired by Spitz's seven gold medals at the 1972 Olympics, I announced that I wanted to take up competitive swimming. Without delay, my father, who stood more than six feet tall and was built like a football player, made a trip to the International Swim Center, introduced himself to Haines, and declared that his daughter would be one of his future champions. "Is she built like you?" Haines asked hopefully. I was undersized, with limbs like sapling branches, but I was unfazed.

Like the kids in Norwich, I grew up rubbing shoulders with, and being taught by, Olympians. Three of my first four coaches had won Olympic medals while training under the charismatic Haines, whose footprint on Santa Clara was equal to the ski coach Walter Prager's at Dartmouth. Those daily interactions with the very best humanized—almost normalized—excellence. Every summer the International Swim Center hosted an invitational, televised by ABC's *Wide World of Sports*, that attracted the best swimmers in the world and produced world-record times. My parents opened our home, less than a mile from the facility, to participating athletes. And so for a single weekend every summer I surrendered my queen-size bed to Olympic medalists like Italy's Novella Calligaris and sat rapt at the dining table listening to their stories. I never did have the opportunity to swim for Haines, who left Santa Clara in 1974 to coach college programs, first at UCLA and later at Stanford. But I was an indirect beneficiary of his charisma, my life set on its course by one of his disciples, Bill Rose.

From his interactions with Haines, Bill would learn enough about swimming to fill an encyclopedia. But the main lessons he took away were about humility and always making time for people. Bill benefited from Haines's generosity of spirit, and he in turn would pay it forward to me when I was thirteen. Toward the end of the eighth grade, my English teacher assigned a project: create a magazine. Mine was called *Splash* and would be anchored by an interview with a swimmer. But which one? To my father, the answer was obvious: Mike Bruner.

Mike was the Michael Phelps of his day, supremely talented in the butterfly, freestyle, and individual medley, and expected to contend for Olympic medals in multiple events at the upcoming 1976 Summer Games. In an era when it was cool for men to wear their hair in feathered mullets, Mike kept his head cleanly shaved, adding to his intimidating aura. Not that it required any reinforcement. He had a reputation for completing training sets that were unfathomable to the rest of us, like averaging under one minute for each 100-yard swim in a 10,000-yard set consisting of 100 x 100-yard freestyles. I had since moved to De Anza Aquatics, where Bill Rose was the head coach, and like all the kids on the team, I was in awe of Mike.

With my father hovering at my side, I approached Bill—always "Coach Rose" to his athletes—and asked, heart in throat, if he thought Mike might be able to spare a few minutes. Rose told me to prepare my questions and stay after practice the next day. He would make sure that Mike talked with me. Decades later, as a reporter with the *New York Times*, I would regularly be reminded of the gift Rose had given me, because most gatekeeper coaches built moats around their athletes and refused to lower the drawbridge.

Rose told Mike he had an interview, and Mike assumed, not unreasonably, that he would be meeting with a reporter from one of the Bay Area dailies. I'm sure he was mortified to be greeted by a pigtailed pip-squeak holding three-by-five index cards in trembling hands. But if Mike was disappointed, he didn't show it. He was gracious with his answers, and my completed magazine earned an A. At my father's suggestion, I made two extra copies for Bill and Mike. I was so excited for them to see that I had earned the highest grade for my efforts—and theirs.

The Olympic trials were held the following month in Long Beach, California, an hour's flight from the Bay Area, and my father took me to the meet. The night before we arrived, Mike failed to make the Olympic team in the 400-meter freestyle. Earlier, he was fourth in the 200 freestyle, missing an individual berth by one spot. Disappointed by the way his meet was unfolding, Mike was in a lousy frame of mind for his best event, the 200 butterfly, which he was swimming on the day we arrived.

I was able to reach the pool deck and deliver a copy of my magazine to Bill, who read my interview as I stood holding my breath. His expression grew animated, and he said, "This is fantastic!" He said he was going to make sure Mike read it right away. He found Mike brooding under the bleachers, handed the magazine to him, and made him read an answer to one of my questions out loud: "I'd say that swimming is at least 90 percent mental. You can work harder than anyone but lose a race because you don't have a positive attitude. The swimmer with the best attitude is the one that will win the race."

Mike, in effect, delivered his own pep talk. He won the 200 butterfly in the final to secure his first individual berth to the Montreal Games. When Mike met with reporters afterward, he was asked how he overcame the disappointments of his earlier races. This was his response, as it appeared in the next day's *Long Beach Press-Telegram*: "A little girl from the club interviewed me for a class project and had gotten an A on the paper.

In it, I talked a lot about hard work, having the will to win and things like that. Reading it brought me back to reality. I think I gave up in the 400 free." The next day, Rose produced a copy of the paper and pointed to the quote, which I read and reread. It was hard for me to grasp that something I had written could have helped Mike make the Olympic team. I turned to my father on the pool deck and told him that I wanted to grow up to tell people's stories for a living.

Mike went on to capture two gold medals in Montreal, including the first of those Games by an American, in the 200 butterfly. And I have covered nearly a dozen Olympics as a sportswriter. With each other's help, we both made our wildest dreams come true.

In 2016, Bill and I were in the audience when Mike was inducted into the San Jose Sports Hall of Fame at SAP Center, home of the NHL's Sharks. The morning after the ceremony, nostalgia pulled me to the swim center renamed in 2002 for Haines. According to USA Swimming, the national governing body for the sport, San Jose and Santa Clara registered six thousand new swimmers in 2016, with more than a third of the athletes signing up in the months leading up to the Rio Games and the weeks after—many no doubt inspired, as I was by Spitz, by Olympic champions like Stanford's Simone Manuel and UC Berkeley's Ryan Murphy.

Blue banners hung on a chain-link fence that separated the pool deck from the spectator seating. They were the Santa Clara Swim Club's version of Norwich's Olympic wall of fame, offering both a nod to the past and a prod for the future. The banners touted the club's decorated history, with its eighty Olympians and fifty-one gold medals, and asked, "Who is next?" It's a good question. The last Santa Clara Swim Club team member to grace a US Olympic team was Tom Wilkens in 2000. It is as if manufacturing Olympic swimmers is just another once-robust industry imperiled by the city's long-established drought cycles. The lengthy gap between homegrown Olympians from Santa Clara reminded me of a quote from a story I read on the efforts by an adjacent county to save nearly a thousand acres of farmland: "Once it's gone, it's gone for good."

Dick Jochums, the head coach who shepherded Wilkens to his bronze medal in the 200-meter individual medley at the Sydney Olympics, considered the final placing the least important aspect of the race. Jochums told me that his philosophy was that the most meaningful victories were not those that resulted in trophies but instead those that occurred when athletes over-came their fears and insecurities to master the moment. But Jochums's views did not find a receptive audience among the tiger moms and tech dads of the swim club, who prize achievement and acquisition. Jochums told me he was left with the distinct impression that most of the parents regarded swimming as valuable in building a résumé, not character.

On the morning I visited the swim center, I found Jochums's successor, John Bitter, standing on the pool deck, putting his swimmers through their paces. Bitter, well-respected by his peers, said it has been a difficult road back to relevance in a city where children have more extracurricular options than ever before—and less free time. Bitter's challenge is to convince busy, results-oriented parents that the intense time commitment—up to five hours a day, six days a week, eleven months a year at the elite level—will pay off in their children developing skills that will ultimately enable them to succeed in the classroom and beyond. A 2015 poll found that more than a quarter of parents of high school athletes hope their offspring will play professional sports. But in sports, exertion can be the enemy of execution—the surest way to fail is to try to succeed. And the numbers clearly aren't in their children's favor. According to the National Collegiate Athletic Association, less than 10 percent of high school athletes will go on to play collegiate sports, and of those, less than 1 percent will be drafted by the NFL, NBA, or MLB.

The Norwich way gives kids ample space to discover their passions and pursue them for their own reasons and at their own pace. Most of the Norwich Olympians pursued part-time work to cover the costs of their sports. As a teenager, the Alpine skier Felix McGrath found a variety of jobs, and while he didn't make much more than minimum wage, the experiences were priceless. "Finding—and keeping—those jobs forced me to be independent and responsible and accountable," Felix said.

The culture created almost by accident in Norwich can be replicated elsewhere, but it requires parents to refrain from micromanaging their children's lives and instead act as their guides to charity, well-roundedness, curiosity, perspective, and a healthy life anchored by physical activity. Their mantra is not "Do as I say, not as I do." The adults in Norwich make a conscious effort to be the people they want their children to become.

That means turning off their technological devices and tuning in to their kids. I attended a high school junior-varsity soccer game in which not a single adult in the stands "watched" with his or her head down while tapping on a smartphone. This was partly due to the fact that cell signals are so weak. But still, the Norwich parents showed me that the line isn't really fine between being present for your children and suffocating them—it can be as wide as the double yellow stripe on a two-way street.

Norwich parents read to their offspring and encourage their interests. They volunteer at their schools and treat sports as a family bonding exercise. They attend their children's activities but they are easy to overlook because they remain in the background. They praise effort, not results, and send a loud and clear message that community trumps competition by embracing the success of children other than their own.

The Norwich parents give their children ownership of their lives. Brook Leigh's mother and father entrust him with coordinating his complicated school schedule directly with his teachers in two states. As a result, he can communicate with adults much better than most teenagers. Julia Krass's parents left it to her to decide whether to finish high school by taking online classes, and because she had taken charge of her education, her sense of accomplishment when she was accepted to Dartmouth was great.

The culture created almost by accident in Norwich also requires coaches to work from the same playbook as the parents. They believe that if they do their jobs right, the kids eventually won't need them. They see themselves as educators, not emissaries assigned to deliver children to the ranks of professional sports.

Proof that the Norwich way can be exported comes from the 1988 Olympian McGrath, who has successfully transplanted it in Norway, where he coaches a club. But it requires teamwork. And it takes people with time, money, or expertise to give freely to fund athletic programs, to find facilities, and to create facsimiles if none exist in towns less blessed than Norwich with its nearby Ivy League campus or Santa Clara with its three-pool swimming facility.

And in urban centers, where mountain trails and swimming pools are not easily accessible, it takes people with time, expertise, and ingenuity to draw children away from their video games and smartphone screens. The Norwich way contains no shortcuts, but then, rearing children to be happy champions and contented, productive adults is worth it.

ACKNOWLEDGMENTS

This book was yoga for my soul, the writing equivalent of a forward bend after what amounts to the long and deep back bend that is my daily existence in the relentlessly male sports journalism world.

The email that ultimately dropped me into the middle of a literary circle of smart, sharp, supportive women. It landed in my *New York Times* inbox when I was at the 2014 Winter Olympics in Sochi, Russia, becoming more despondent by the day because of the disappearing stray dogs whose faces all reminded me of Cobber, my beloved toy Australian shepherd, and the vanishing Olympic ideals that had drawn me to sports in the first place.

I had heard about a tiny town in Vermont from which US Olympians flowed like maple syrup? It didn't matter that I had never stepped foot in Vermont and had never written a book: Alia Hanna Habib, a literary agent at McCormick Literary, instilled in me the confidence that I could do it. From proposal to completed manuscript, she was the best coach I've ever had. A nod also to Alia's colleague Bridget McCarthy for walking me through various technical labyrinths.

My good fortune continued with this project landing in the capable hands of Priscilla Painton of Simon & Schuster, whose 1992 *Time* magazine cover story on Ted Turner inspired me to be a better, more empathetic journalist. Early in the writing process, Priscilla tossed me a piece of advice that I would cling to like a life preserver: never lose sight of the fact that no matter whose story you're telling, Norwich is the main character.

Priscilla's assistant, Megan Hogan, was invaluable. I lost count of the number of times she saved me. Their Simon & Schuster colleague Jessica Chin and copyeditor Stephanie Evans copyedited the book with tender loving care and were the perfect midwives for the final push to delivery. You never know from where inspiration will spring; Deirdre Heekin's reading at the Norwich Bookstore inspired my epiphany that the athletes are developed much like the crops in the area. So thank you, Deirdre, for unwittingly nurturing this project.

While researching this book, I came across a notecard designed by the Middlebury artist Nancie Dunn that read "What happens in Vermont stays in Vermont. But not much really happens. And that's the way we like it." Such a little state, so much humility and self-deprecation! The most challenging part of this project was convincing the Olympians that their stories were interesting. A heartfelt thank-you to Sunny Snite, Mike and Jeff and Chris Hastings, and, Jim Holland, who had similar reactions when I first contacted them: basically, "I don't know why you would want to talk to me." Neither did Brett Heyl, Hannah Kearney, Julia Krass, Brook Leigh, Tim Tetreault, and Andrew Wheating, who nonetheless suffered graciously my repeated visits, phone calls, emails, and texts. To my everlasting gratitude, they treated me like an honorary Vermonter.

The Norwich Historical Society has archives that I spent entire days happily poring through. A special thanks to Sarah Rooker and Bill Aldrich for being my guides. I conducted many of my interviews at the Norwich landmark King Arthur Flour. The first time I arranged to meet someone there, I bought a meal for a man in a Boston Red Sox cap who waited until he had polished off his chocolate croissant before telling me he was not Andrew Wheating's first track coach, Jeff Johnson, but a trucker meeting a blind date for breakfast.

To Jeff and all the parents and others who opened their homes, their hearts, and, in at least one case, their Olympic journal to me, I'm deeply appreciative. To Rusty Sachs and the dozens of people I met who supplied pieces of information that helped me complete the puzzle that is Norwich's grand Olympic tradition, this book's for you.

When I was struggling with the proposal, a group of fierce, fun, and fabulous women I met at a leadership conference in Boise came to the rescue. Led by Anne Taylor Fleming, they've provided encouragement I can never repay.

A heartfelt thank-you to Liza Bernard, Peter Carlisle, Jeff Johnson, Patty LaDuca, Berta Ledecky, Teresa Oster, Allison Wagner, and Lisa Wagner, whose constructive feedback on various drafts helped make the final product infinitely better. And to Michael Salmon of the LA84 Foundation library, LA's best-kept secret, for his research expertise.

If not for Tim Buke, I probably never would have crossed the radar of Tom Jolly, who hired me at the *New York Times*. I'm indebted to them, to Jason Stallman, whose faith and trust I never take for granted, and to others who are always there to lend a hand or a handkerchief, a group that includes but is not limited to: David Adler, Bruce Anderson, Ken Belson, Paola Boivin, Liz Clarke, Joe Drape, Anne Geers, Terri Ann Glynn, Mikki Johnson, Sandy Keenan, Teri McKeever, Gwen Knapp, Craig and Pammie Neff, Carl Nelson, Tracy Pennea, Ron Rapoport, Karen and Kevin Riggs, Tom Rinaldi, David Robinson, Robin Scholefield, and Shelley Smith.

Finally, I want to recognize my mom, Patricia Crouse, who fostered my love of books by reading to me every night without fail when I was young; my sister, Christie Gonyer, for her forbearance; my father, James Crouse, who would have bragged endlessly to his cronies (and anyone else who crossed his path) about this book if he had lived to see it published; and my husband, Roderic Millie, who took care of all the little things so I was free to tackle this big project and who makes home my favorite destination.

NOTES

PROLOGUE

1   *with its roughly 1,440 single-family households*: Jonathan Bynum, finance assistant for Town of Norwich, email to author, January 27, 2017.

3   *Spain, with its population of 46 million*: David Wallechinsky, *The Complete Book of the Winter Olympics*, 2014 ed. (New York: Crossroad Press, 2013); page verified by Dr. Bill Mallon of the International Society of Olympic Historians, email to author, March 2, 2017.

3   *New Zealand, home to 4.7 million people*: Ibid.

3   *"I don't know if it's the well water or what"*: Charles McGrath, "Turning Her Fear Upside Down," *New York Times*, February 16, 2010.

4   *a median household income of eighty-nine thousand dollars*: http://www.city-data.com/city/Norwich-Vermont.html.

4   *The father of Norwich's first summer Olympian*: Mike Heyl, telephone interview by author, January 4, 2017.

5   *favors autonomy over relationships*: Niobe Way, lunch interview by author, Le Pain Quotidien, New York City, November 21, 2016.

6   *a saying passed down through the generations*: Vanessa Wolff, lunch interview by author, Sabai Sabai, Middlebury, Vermont, November 9, 2016.

6   *Forty percent of the group*: Benedict Carey, "After Glory of a Lifetime, Asking 'What Now?'" *New York Times*, August 18, 2008.

7   *Jim Kenyon, a columnist for the local* Valley News: Jim Kenyon, telephone interview by author, September 26, 2016.

7   *the town's unofficial den mother*: Beth Reynolds, lunch interview by author, Books-a-Million, West Lebanon, New Hampshire, November 23, 2015.

7   *the first Games to be televised live in the United States*: David C. Antonucci, *Snowball's Chance: The Story of the 1960 Winter Games Squaw Valley & Lake Tahoe* (Lake Tahoe: Art of Learning Publishing, 2009), 54.

8   *NBC showed fifteen hundred hours*: NBC Universal press release, February 25, 2014.

9   *progressed from "a flying sack of potatoes"*: Jeff Hastings, interview by author, Norwich Inn, October 30, 2015.

10   *On an Internet community board*: Lee Michaelides, "Mary Poppins Riles Norwich," *Daily UV*, January 14, 2016.

10   *Norwich is a place with deep agrarian roots*: *Norwich, Vermont: A History* (Norwich, Vermont: The Norwich Historical Society, 2012), 6.

12   *Nearly three years after her Olympic gold-medal performance*:
      Hannah Kearney, email to author, February 28, 2017.

12   *She returned to competition three months after the October 2012
      accident*: Ibid.

12   *their drive was summed up by Hannah*: Hannah Kearney, break-
      fast interview by author, Bandana's Grill, Park City, Utah, April
      22, 2016.

12   *In 1960, when Betsy Snite*: Wallechinsky, 2.

13   *the program had grown*: https://www.olympic.org/sochi-2014.

13   *I attended a reading*: Deirdre Heekin, *An Unlikely Vineyard:
      The Education of a Farmer and Her Quest for Terroir* (White
      River Junction, Vermont: Chelsea Green Publishing, 2014);
      reading by Deirdre Heekin, Norwich Bookstore, October 29,
      2014.

13   *focused on the five factors*: Ibid.

14   *And while the families have shrunk*: Andrew Crabtree of the City
      of Santa Clara, email to author, December 9, 2016.

14   *as one old-timer said with a sniff*: Interview by author, West
      Boylston, Massachusetts, October 27, 2015.

16   *ex-jocks, like the father I met*: Clayton Simmers, interview by
      author, Huntley Meadow, Norwich, Vermont, September 12,
      2015.

19   *The gathering spot has served*: Dan Fraser, telephone interview
      by author, March 8, 2017.

20   *Goodrich Hill, Sadler's Hill, Lyle Field*: Norwich, Vermont, 208.

21   *who chose her outfit for school*: Hannah Kearney, lunch inter-
      view by author, Norwich Inn, Norwich, Vermont, October 30,
      2014.

21   *Tetreault teamed with a dozen of his classmates*: Tim Tetreault,

breakfast interview by author, the Metro Diner, Arlington, Virginia, December 8, 2016.

23   *during one of my visits*: David Corriveau, "A Path for Every Student; Hanover High Plans for a Less Pressurized Atmosphere," *Valley News*, October 28, 2014.

24   *The president of the*: "TSG Consumer Partners Acquires Backcountry," TSG Consumer Partners press release, July 1, 2015.

25   *rolled up a record tab*: David Segal, "Now What? A City Fears a Flameout," *New York Times*, February 24, 2014.

CHAPTER 1: SKI PATROL

29   *She hadn't been back to Norwich*: Sunny Snite, lunch interview by author, Caffe Firenze, Florence, Montana, June 10, 2015.

30   *Like the alcohol on Betsy's breath in her later years*: Penny Pitou, lunch interview by author, O Steaks and Seafood, Laconia, New Hampshire, October 29, 2015.

30   *He was the epitome of the parent . . . pushing his kids"*: Heyl interview.

30   *"Al would have been better off"*: Dick Colton, telephone interview by author, September 14, 2015.

30   *"I wanted the horses more than the skiing"*: Sunny Snite, interviews by author, Norwich, Vermont, October 24 through November 3, 2015.

32   *Dartmouth College, which in 1928 hosted*: outdoors.darthmouth .edu/doc/history.html.

32   *Ford Sayre, a Dartmouth graduate*: Lois Friedland, "Ford Sayre's Idea," *Skiing*, December 1978, 232E.

NOTES

33   *"He wanted them to become the next Andrea Mead Lawrence"*: Heyl interview.

34   *"I was a little blessed"*: Elizabeth Edgerton, telephone interview by author, September 23, 2016.

35   *She was all smiles*: "Ski Queen Throws Snow Ball," *Seventeen*, January 1960, 70–71.

35   *"17-year-old member"*: Ibid.

35   *sat next to Sunny at a different table decades later*: Elise Braestrup Wellington, interview by author, West Boylston, Massachusetts, October 27, 2015.

37   *"Bend zee knees, two dollars, please"*: Patricia L. Haslam, Charlie Lord, and Sepp Ruschp, *Ski Pioneers of Stowe, Vermont: The First Twenty-Five Years* (iUniverse LLC, 2013), 247.

38   *The local children would return empty soda bottles at Merrill's General Store*: Wellington interview.

39   *Al and Betty radiated wealth*: Wellington, telephone interview by author, April 28, 2017.

39   *On Dartmouth alumni forms*: Rauner Special Collections Library, Dartmouth College, October 29, 2015.

40   *A woman who grew up near the Snites*: Lois Porter, conversation during dinner for Sunny Snite in Norwich, Vermont, October 25, 2015.

41   *Years later, Sunny would read aloud a quote from Betsy*: Sunny's visit to the Norwich Historical Society, October 30, 2015.

42   *"quite a taskmaster"*: Jim Kenyon, "Ford Sayre Award Plaque in Her Name: Remembering Betsy Snite," *Valley News*, April 6, 1985.

42   *"Dad told me . . . he'd take my skis away"*: Ibid.

42   *"a ballerina on skis"*: Sachs, conversation.

NOTES

43 *Betsy's friend and rival . . . "the last of the small Olympics"*: Pitou interview.

43 *After Pitou won her second silver . . . only to be cornered by then Vice President*: Ibid.

44 *"an ardent and often very vocal ski fan"*: Ibid.

44 *"When it's time to race, I'll be ready"*: Roy Terrell, "Those Pretty Girls with the Killer Instinct," *Sports Illustrated*, February 1, 1960, 34–37.

45 *"She was probably the best . . . I've ever skied with"*: Pitou interview.

45 *the skiers referred to Betsy affectionately as their mascot*: Rusty Sachs, conversation during dinner for Sunny Snite in Norwich, Vermont, October 25, 2015.

45 *In a 2000 interview*: Michael Schulman, *Her Again: Becoming Meryl Streep* (New York: HarperCollins, 2016), 49.

46 *Once, Penny said*: Pitou interview, October 29, 2015.

46 *it definitely calmed her nerves*: Pia Riva McIsaac, email to author, October 12, 2016.

48 *"Betsy did everything her father wanted"*: Joan Hannah, telephone interview by author, September 24, 2016.

48 *Then I showed her a newspaper clipping*: Sunny Snite, interview by author, The Norwich Historical Society, October 30, 2015, while looking at an article by Art Ballou, "Slalom Queen Betsy Snite Learned Skiing in Back Yard," *Valley News*, April 5, 1959.

51 *"You learn to ski fast"*: Terrell, "Those Pretty Girls with the Killer Instinct."

51 *Josl pleaded with her to stop drinking*: Josl Rieder, email to author facilitated by Unser Loisach, September 17, 2016.

52   *"She was just floundering"*: Pitou interview.

52   *Betsy was among the honored invitees*: Janet Nelson, "The Ski Tow Is 50 Years Old," *New York Times*, January 9, 1984.

52   *Bill said that it was common knowledge*: Bill Aldrich, interview by author, The Norwich Historical Society, Norwich, Vermont, October 30, 2014.

53   *Imagine, Elizabeth said*: Edgerton interview.

54   *"I didn't know her really well"*: Marilyn Cochran Brown, Vermont Sports Hall of Fame banquet, Double Tree by Hilton, Burlington, Vermont, April 22, 2017.

55   *"I could finally give . . . while she was still alive"*: Sunny Snite, text message to author, April 8, 2017.

58   *"And then all of a sudden . . . you disappeared"*: Porter, conversation.

61   *Her daughter . . . witnessed the abuse meted out*: Maria Lyle, text message to author, April 22, 2017.

64   *Mike remembered Al being overbearing*: Heyl interview.

65   *After Betsy's husband died . . . custodians of their memories*: Karin Gottlieb, telephone interview by author, April 23, 2017.

65   *In 1971, in a personal letter to a friend*: Rauner Special Collections, Dartmouth College, Ford Sayre Memorial Ski Council files.

66   *Dagny would later say of her swimming . . . a passenger along for the ride*: Karen Crouse, "A Former Top Swimmer Gives Happiness a Chance," *New York Times*, January 26, 2013.

CHAPTER 2: NORWICH'S AIR FORCE

69   *Mike Holland stood in the gymnasium at Marion Cross*: Mike Holland, ski jumping presentation to schoolchildren, Marion Cross Elementary School, Norwich, Vermont, January 14, 2016.

72   *He flew 186 meters*: E. John B. Allen, *Historical Dictionary of Skiing* (Toronto: Scarecrow Press, 2012), 211.

74   *He advocates the same generalized approach*: Felix McGrath, emails to author, February 3 and 4, 2017.

76   "*'God that was scary'*": Mike Holland, interview by author, Norwich Inn, Norwich, Vermont, October 31, 2014.

77   *They argued that it was stunting the sport's growth*: Jeff Hastings, interview by author, October 30, 2014.

77   *Barbara, who was terrified of heights:* Harry and Barbara Holland, dinner interview by author, Jesse's, Hanover, New Hampshire, September 12, 2015.

78   "*It was really unique*": Chris Hastings, interview by author at his chiropractic office, Norwich, Vermont, October 28, 2015.

79   "*That thrill . . . it's what brought me back*": Tetreault interview.

79   *enhance not only performance but also physical and emotional well-being*: Tara Parker-Pope, "What Are Friends For? A Longer Life," *New York Times*, April 20, 2009.

80   *Early on, Mike could match Jeff's work ethic if not his results*: Holland interview.

81   *Jim Holland set the one-way record*: Jim Holland, interview by author, Starbucks, Park City, Utah, January 8, 2015.

83   "*Mike was a lot of raw talent . . . elegant ski jumper*": Jeff Hastings interview.

83   *Mike learned to be creative in how he solicited money*: Mike Holland, email to author, January 30, 2017.

84   *In 2007, the US Ski and Snowboard Association discontinued its financial support for the sport*: Alan Johnson, USA Nordic Sports Board of Directors, telephone interview by author, June 14, 2017.

85   *veteran farmers helped their neighbors starting out*: Heekin reading.

86   *the poem penned by Polly Forcier*: Polly Forcier, email to author, November 5, 2014.

88   *"We kept hearing for years . . . and a lot of people did"*: Mike Holland interview.

89   *"Everyone looked at me like we're done, he's going to be the one"*: Brett Heyl, telephone interview by author, April 29, 2017.

89   *Ask him about his brush with history*: Jeff Hastings interview.

92   *"It was like he had read my mind"*: Tetreault interview.

92   *He joked that the program could use "three or four more" Hollands*: Harry and Barbara Holland interview.

93   *"It just flips a switch in your head"*: Jim Holland interview.

94   *Fifty percent of the track athletes*: Jere Longman, "Nick Symmonds, a Polarizing Force in Track and Field, Announces Retirement Plans," *New York Times*, January 4, 2017.

95   *averaged less than twenty thousand in most years*: Tetreault interview.

95   *"If you continue doing something . . . can't really grow in other ways"*: Karen Crouse, "After Moguls Come Life's Bumps," *New York Times*, January 14, 2015.

96   *"the world's best job and the world's worst career"*: Chris Hastings interview.

98   *"The sport continues to give me far more than I could ever repay"*: Jeff Hastings interview.

CHAPTER 3: HOSANNAS FOR HANNAH

106 *Her parents had bought the house in foreclosure*: Tom Kearney, interview by author, November 12, 2015.

107 *At five months, she could stand on the palm*: Hannah Kearney and Jill Kearney Niles, lunch interview by author, Norwich Inn, Norwich, Vermont, October 30, 2014.

111 *Jill will sit down with the offender*: Jill Kearney Niles, series of interviews by author, Norwich, Vermont, fall of 2015.

111 *"It takes me a long time to warm up to people"*: Hannah Kearney interview, April 22, 2016.

112 *"There was talk about her playing high school soccer like no other guy . . . at Hanover High"*: Jeff Hastings interview.

112 *Hannah walked into class on the first day*: Wendy Thompson, interview by author, Marion Cross Elementary School, Norwich, Vermont, November 10, 2016.

114 *She kept meticulous training logs*: Hannah Kearney, interview by author, Park City, Utah, January 7, 2015.

115 *She graced the medals podium*: Greg Fennell, "A Champion's Next Challenge; At 29, Norwich's Hannah Kearney Makes the Leap Into Retirement," *Valley News*, April 18, 2015.

117 *"You don't find people . . . not giving back"*: Hannah Kearney interview, April 22, 2016.

121 *children held up handmade signs that read "Hannah Hustles"*: Greg Fennell, "It's Off to Turin: Kearney Gets an Olympic Send-Off," *Valley News*, January 18, 2006.

122 *"No one said, 'Oh, we're so sorry,' . . . that was fantastic"*: Hannah Kearney and Jill Kearney Niles interview.

NOTES

123 *Hannah, who once bet Denny a hundred dollars that he wouldn't . . . fight an opponent*: Hannah Kearney interview.

125 *Hannah had another medal, shaped like the state*: Hannah Kearney, email to author, March 3, 2017.

125 *Back in Norwich, the townspeople decided a celebration was in order*: Dan Barry, "For a Moment of Glory, Mastering a Million Details," *New York Times*, February 28, 2010.

126 *She asked the children's librarian*: Reynolds interview.

126 *Hannah made more than a quarter of a million dollars*: Hannah Kearney interview, January 7, 2015.

128 *Hannah was described as "the closest thing there is to a sure thing on snow"*: "Hannah's Heartbreaker," Associated Press, February 9, 2014.

130 *Riordan sewed banners*: Molly Riordan, interview by author, Norwich Square Café, Norwich, Vermont, November 10, 2016.

131 *The microphone burbled with static*: Ibid.

CHAPTER 4: SETTING HIS OWN PACE

135 *Jeff Johnson could not believe he had been coaxed out of hibernation*: Jeff Johnson, interview by author, King Arthur Flour, Norwich, Vermont, September 9, 2015.

136 *"Hopeless, just hopeless"*: Ibid.

137 *He took the shoving personally*: Andrew Wheating, interview by author, Vero Café, Eugene, Oregon, May 31, 2015.

138 *They believed that children mature*: Betsy and Justin Wheating, breakfast interview by author, Norwich Inn, Norwich, Vermont, October 31, 2015.

139 *Andrew's paternal grandmother*: Ibid.

140 *studied by the psychologist Benjamin Bloom*: Adam Grant, "How to Raise a Creative Child. Step One: Back Off," *New York Times*, January 31, 2016.

141 *"That should have been the first sign"*: Andrew Wheating interview.

142 *"I just knew if he stayed . . . he'd float to the bottom"*: Betsy and Justin Wheating, telephone interview by author, February 8, 2017.

143 *a pace unattainable by all but roughly 10 percent*: Johnson interview.

143 *"It's not like we invested in Andy . . . an Olympian"*: Kevin Ramos-Glew, interview by author, Kimball Union Academy, Plainfield, New Hampshire, December 2, 2015.

144 *He once held the American record*: Steve Prefontaine biography, National Track & Field Hall of Fame, Indianapolis, Indiana.

145 *for the company that in 1971 became Nike*: Matt McCue, "Employee Number One," *Runner's World*, February 26, 2013, http://www .runnersworld.com/masters/employee-number-one.

146 *"It was terribly risky"*: Johnson interview.

147 *"Where's Jeff Johnson?"*: Jeff Johnson interview, King Arthur Flour, Norwich, Vermont, November 11, 2016.

151 *One of the United States' leading experts on youth sports injuries*: David Epstein, "Sports Should Be Child's Play," *New York Times*, June 11, 2014.

152 *Andrew would later be described*: Kenny Moore, "Out of Nowhere," *Runner's World*, August 18, 2009, http://www.runnersworld .com/runners-stories/andrew-wheatings-running-story.

153 *The Norwegian Grete Waitz*: Liz Robbins and Bruce Weber,

"Grete Waitz, Marathon Champion, Dies at 57," *New York Times*, April 20, 2011.

154 *offered him a two-hundred-dollar athletic scholarship*: Vin Lananna, telephone interview by author, October 27, 2016.

157 *A record 20,939 spectators had crammed*: Scott M. Reid, "Oregonians Sweep Wild 800-Meters," *Orange County Register*, June 30, 2008, http://www.ocregister.com/2008/06/30/oregonians -sweep-wild-800-meters.

159 *Andrew wouldn't know "a steroid from a hemorrhoid"*: Johnson interview, November 11, 2016.

160 *The send-off embodied what he loved about the town*: Andrew Wheating interview.

161 *one of the first interstate school districts in the country*: http://www. hanoverchamber.org/elbo/assets/2AboutHanoverNorwich.pdf.

163 *"The material things . . . it's all temporary"*: Andrew Wheating interview.

164 *At the 2010 NCAA Outdoor Track and Field Championships*: Greg Fennell, "Leaving Amateurs Behind; Norwich's Wheating Is Dominant, but He Aims Higher," *Valley News*, July 30, 2010.

167 *"I sit there and wonder . . . the innocence of just purely running is so clear"*: Andrew Wheating interview.

168 *describe running as a business and "a great way for me to market my products"*: Longman, "Nick Symmonds, a Polarizing Force in Track and Field, Announces Retirement Plans."

169 *His need for community compelled him to join*: Andrew Wheating, telephone interview by author, October 24, 2016.

171 *"I'm not making the teams and . . . they're cutting me down further and further"*: Ibid.

CHAPTER 5: FREEDOM RIDER

174 *His family didn't own a car*: Pia and Simon Pearce, lunch interview by author, Simon Pearce Restaurant, Quechee, Vermont, December 16, 2015.

175 *replete with a sleeping loft . . . and a skateboard ramp in the back*: John Branch, "A Snowboarder's Dream and a Family's Anguish," *New York Times*, January 5, 2010.

176 *They intuitively sensed what a 2013 study . . . showed*: H. H. Schiffrin et al. (2013), "Helping or Hovering? The Effects of Helicopter Parenting on College Students' Well-Being," *Journal of Child and Family Studies* 23, no. 3 (April 2014): 548–57; DOI 10.1007/s10826-013-9716-3.

176 *He told me about meeting Jeff's commercial flight home*: Paul Hastings, telephone interview by author, October 6, 2014.

179 *"He got to spend the best part of the day outside"*: Pia Pearce, telephone interview by author, February 9, 2017.

180 *He gave them credit for the heights*: Kevin Pearce, interview by author, San Diego, California, December 16, 2016.

180 *"but it never felt reckless . . . always very controlled"*: Drake Naples, telephone interview by author, November 17, 2016.

180 *Studies have shown that some people have a genetic variant*: Alex Hutchinson, "What Makes Extreme Athletes Take Risks?" *Globe and Mail*, March 9, 2014.

181 *As boys prepare to strike out on their own*: Way interview.

182 *the less steep they perceived the*: Parker-Pope, "What Are Friends For?"

182 *They called themselves the "frends"*: Matt Higgins, "For a Group

of Snowboarding Pals, There's No 'I' in Friends," *New York Times*, March 21, 2009.

183   *"My goal is to make people . . . 'try that'"*: Shira Springer, "Perilous Pursuit," *Boston Globe*, January 8, 2010.

183   *he crashed and sustained a concussion, at least the fourth of his career*: Pia Pearce interview.

184   *"All the pressure was on me . . . So I got up there, I kept riding"*: Ibid.

185   *He spent ten days in a coma*: Reuven Blau, "Former Top-Ranked Snowboarder Kevin Pearce to Speak About His Recovery to Students and Seniors in Brooklyn Heights," *New York Daily News*, September 22, 2014.

185   *whose own competitive career had been cut short four years earlier*: Adam Pearce, email to author, February 1, 2017.

185   *"It amazed me . . . 'new goals to conquer'"*: Adam Pearce interview.

185   *"You're an Olympic Hero in Our Hearts"*: Barry, "For a Moment of Glory."

186   *"The support was unbelievable"*: Pia and Simon Pearce interview.

186   *Kevin returned to his snowboard 712 days after the accident*: Eddie Pells, "Sun Shines on the Mountain and Pearce Rides Again," *San Diego Union-Tribune*, December 13, 2011.

186   *Simon . . . blamed himself for Kevin's accident*: Pia and Simon Pearce interview.

187   *Simon said in* The Crash Reel: Lucy Walker and Pedros Kos, *The Crash Reel,* directed by Lucy Walker, 2013.

187   *wishes she had educated herself earlier about concussions*: Pia Pearce interview.

188   *"I would do that piece dramatically different"*: Ibid.

188 *"That movie's hard for me to watch"*: Kevin Pearce, interview by author, Arizona Science Center, Phoenix, Arizona, April 21, 2017.

190 *a year later at a San Diego, California, fund-raiser*: Love Your Brain Foundation fund-raiser at Casa del Balboa, San Diego, California, December 16, 2016.

191 *sustained a traumatic brain injury while seated on an airplane*: Pia Pearce interview.

192 *He emerged from the accident a better person*: Pia and Simon Pearce interview.

192 *"Before, I wasn't doing anything important . . . I wasn't helping that many people"*: Kevin Pearce interview, December 16, 2016.

192 *"There's a lot more to life than landing a trick"*: Kevin Pearce, interview by author, Simon Pearce Store, Quechee, Vermont, November 29, 2015.

CHAPTER 6: THE FUTURE OF NORWICH

198 *"The madness had to stop"*: Peter Krass, telephone interview by author, December 8, 2016.

198 *I met Julia on the soccer pitch in the fall of 2014*: Julia Krass, interview by author, Hanover High School, Hanover, New Hampshire, October 31, 2014.

203 *"All I can do is what I know how to do, so I might as well go for it"*: Ibid.

203 *and then scrambled to renew her passport and obtain a visa*: Peter Krass interview.

204 *"There are no expectations or pressure . . . enjoy representing your*

country on this world stage": Jared Pendak, "Hanover Teen Krass Thrilled for Surprise Berth," *Valley News*, January 22, 2014.

204 *A student-made banner was hung in the Hanover High cafeteria*: Doug Alden, "Hanover Watches," *Union Leader*, February 12, 2014.

204 *President Obama remarked on her youthfulness*: Julia Krass interview.

205 *a fourteen-year-old snowboarder became the youngest X Games gold medalist*: Jason Blevins, "Teen Skier Kelly Sildaru Becomes Youngest X Games Gold Medalist," *Denver Post*, January 29, 2016.

206 *as Julia lined up for her attempt—which she converted—the crowd broke into a chant of "U-S-A"*: Jimmy Golen, "Olympic Skier Krass Wins High School Soccer Title," Associated Press, November 11, 2014.

206 *landed hard, and tore the ACL and meniscus in her right knee*: Julia Krass, interview by author, Starbucks, Hanover, New Hampshire, December 21, 2015.

207 *"Almost everyone tears their ACL at one time or another"*: Ibid.

208 *"My sport is very spontaneous . . . I really like that"*: Julia Krass interview, October 31, 2014.

209 *"It's a little more rough-and-tumble"*: Peter Krass interview.

209 *his ultimate dream is to return to Norwich someday*: Brett Heyl interview.

209 *He quickly tired of people saying, in parting, "Have a nice day"*: Chris Hastings interview.

210 *a thief had stolen a row of organic broccoli*: Jennifer Costa, "Vt. Police Search for Broccoli Thief," WCAX, November 6, 2014,

http://www.wcax.com/story/27320594/vt-police-search-for-broccoli-thief.

211   *"You'd get to know people . . . That's not the case anymore"*: Hannah Kearney interview.

211   *the townspeople pooled their resources and chartered a bus to New York*: Kenyon interview.

211   *A few neighbors carpooled to the event*: Jill Kearney Niles, interview by author, Norwich, Vermont, November 9, 2016.

212   *"people you otherwise wouldn't get to know"*: Brook Leigh, interview by author, Norwich, Vermont, September 12, 2015.

212   *The first time I talked to him was shortly before his sixteenth birthday*: Ibid.

214   *"I like being in the wilderness"*: Ibid.

214   *The force of the landing shredded ligaments in his left knee, requiring surgery*: Brook Leigh, telephone interview by author, November 1, 2016.

214   *"I love what I'm doing . . . than I would from playing it safe"*: Ibid.

215   *"an unnatural sport that teaches a lot of life lessons, like confronting fear"*: Mike Holland presentation.

EPILOGUE

218   *Santa Clara grower named Levi A. Gould shipped*: "Santa Clara 'The Mission City': A Brief History of Santa Clara," City of Santa Clara website, http://santaclaraca.gov/about/city-history/the-mission-city.

218   *"Get it started, get it sold, and move on"*: Steve Ballmer, address to MBA students, University of Southern California, March 10, 2015.

NOTES

219   *Spitz was one of fifteen club members*: USA Swimming archives of Olympic team rosters, confirmed by Chris von Saltza Olmstead, manager for the 1968 US Olympic swim team, interview by author, Sacramento, April 27, 2017.

223   *This was his response*: Gary Rausch, "Bruner Lives Up to Notices," *Long Beach Press-Telegram*, June 20, 1976.

225   *Jochums told me that his philosophy*: Dick Jochums, telephone interview by author, November 2, 2016.

226   *A 2015 poll*: K. J. Dell'Antonia, "Odds Are, Your Sport-Playing Child Isn't Going Pro. Now What?" *New York Times*, September 8, 2015.

227   *less than 10 percent of high school athletes*: Ibid.

227   *"Finding—and keeping—those jobs . . . responsible and accountable"*: McGrath emails.

INDEX

INDEX

ABOUT THE AUTHOR

Karen Crouse has been a *New York Times* staff writer since 2005. This is her first book. She lives in Phoenix.